The Complete PowerXL Air Fryer Grill Cookbook

Easy, Quick, Affordable PowerXL Air Fryer Recipes to Fry, Bake, Grill & Roast for Family Meals Any Time

Larien Riando

Copyright© 2020 By Larien Riando All Rights Reserved

The content contained within this book may not be reproduced, duplicated or transmitted without direct written permission from the author or the publisher.

Under no circumstances will any blame or legal responsibility be held against the publisher, or author, for any damages, reparation, or monetary loss due to the information contained within this book, either directly or indirectly.

Legal Notice:

This book is copyright protected. It is only for personal use. You cannot amend, distribute, sell, use, quote or paraphrase any part, or the content within this book, without the consent of the author or publisher.

Disclaimer Notice:

Please note the information contained within this document is for educational and entertainment purposes only. All effort has been executed to present accurate, up to date, reliable, complete information. No warranties of any kind are declared or implied. Readers acknowledge that the author is not engaged in the rendering of legal, financial, medical or professional advice. The content within this book has been derived from various sources. Please consult a licensed professional before attempting any techniques outlined in this book.

By reading this document, the reader agrees that under no circumstances is the author responsible for any losses, direct or indirect, that are incurred as a result of the use of the information contained within this document, including, but not limited to, errors, omissions, or inaccuracies.

CONTETNE

1 Introduction

9   **Chapter 1** Staples
13   **Chapter 2** Breakfasts
23   **Chapter 3** Fish and Seafood
32   **Chapter 4** Meats
42   **Chapter 5** Poultry
52   **Chapter 6** Vegan and Vegetarian
61   **Chapter 7** Vegetable Sides
66   **Chapter 8** Appetizers and Snacks
71   **Chapter 9** Desserts
77   **Chapter 10** Casseroles, Frittata, and Quiche
83   **Chapter 11** Wraps and Sandwiches
89   **Chapter 12** Holiday Specials
97   **Chapter 13** Fast and Easy Everyday Favorites
104 **Chapter 14** Rotisserie Recipes

109 Appendix 1 Measurement Conversion Chart
110 Appendix 2 Air Fryer Cooking Chart
112 Appendix 3 Recipe Index

Introduction

As someone who loves cooking and eating delicious recipes, I make sure that I do not skip any new kitchen appliance in the market. So, when I first learned about the PowerXL Air Fryer Grill, I was ecstatic. Since I have used several other products by PowerXL in the past, I knew that it would also be worth trying. So, I immediately went to the store and brought home the wonderful PowerXL Air Fryer Grill. Trust me, even after months of using it, I just can't get enough!

This air fryer-cum-grill is not only multi-functional, but it is aesthetically pleasing as well. Just seeing it on my countertop makes me want to keep cooking. Well, I can't help it!

It comes with different presets that make cooking an easy-breezy task. On top of that, multiple accessories can be used to bring all your recipes to life. Whether my husband is cooking the food or me, we hardly see any mess in the kitchen. Thanks to PowerXL! You can easily remove the attachments and wash them separately without creating any mess.

Therefore, considering my experience with PowerXL Air Fryer Grill, I decided to compile 500 recipes that can be cooked using this wonderful kitchen appliance. Besides, in this cookbook, there is other important information that you can use whenever you decide to cook with PowerXL Air Fryer Grill.

Usage

The most important part of any cooking appliance is its usage. You need to be aware of how it functions and what all you can make from it. Honestly, I was a little nervous before trying the PowerXL Air Fryer Grill, but as soon as I started putting it to use, my life changed. I love to cook, especially for my family and friends, and by including this amazing appliance in my kitchen, I could cook even more effortlessly!

Let me show you some of the functions offered by the PowerXL Air Fryer Grill.

Air fry

The air fryer function of this oven doesn't really deep-fry food. Instead, it acts as a hot chamber that cooks food using the air inside the appliance. The food gets cooked at a faster speed and more evenly than a pan. Therefore, you can easily save a lot of time and cook multiple things at once.

With the air fryer function, you can cook packaged food with much more ease. Apart from that, you can also prepare meals right from scratch. Another thing that I love the most about this function is that it keeps food like steak, chicken breasts, and lamb juicy and tender. But that's not all it offers; you can also cook vegetables. Just put a small amount of olive oil, and you are good to go!

Grill

Grilling refers to cooking food on a rack over a heat source. This heat source is usually charcoal or ceramic briquettes. Seems like a task, huh? But wait, here is a simple way to grill your favorite food - PowerXL Air Fryer Grill! After placing the food inside the oven, use the grill function, and cook flavored and crusty delicacies.

Besides, you can roast chicken, corn, tomato, eggplants, and more with the help of this function. On top of that, when the food is cooked over moderate heat, it will gain a smokier taste. Yum!

Rotisserie

The rotisserie function of PowerXL Air Fryer Grill can be used to cook the meat of chicken, turkey, pig, and lamb. Besides, you can also cook beef roasts on a rotisserie.

In this function, the meat is placed on a rotisserie unit. Upon pressing the start button, the unit begins rotation. The steady speed of rotation ensures that the meat gets cooked both internally and externally. In addition to that, it produces exceptional succulence and moistness. The fat that drips from the meat gets collected in the dripping tray. Therefore, making sure that the oven remains clean from the inside.

Bake

Honestly, if it wasn't for this amazing appliance by PowerXL, I could not have made some of the yummiest desserts for my family! With the bake function, you can easily make cookies, cakes, bread, brownies, patties, doughnuts, and more. Besides, even your kids will be able to try out new recipes with ease.

But first, you will have to preheat the oven as per the requirement of the recipe. Just make sure that you or anyone else using this function does not overheat the oven, or else your much-awaited recipe will not turn out as you want. Happy baking!

Roast

Just like the grilling feature, roasting is a method of cooking food using heat. The hot air from the oven surrounds the food and makes sure it gets cooked evenly on all sides. However, there is one difference. While grilling cooks the food faster, roasting cooks the food slowly. Therefore, I would recommend you to roast a bigger piece of food with this function.

It is a great way to bring out the extra flavor of any recipe and give the food a crispy brown color. Therefore, if you want to relax after a tiring day, let this appliance take the lead!

Pizza

Pizza is a great snack idea that will fill up your tummy in seconds. Plus, it is even better when you can make it in just a few easy steps.

With the PowerXL Air Fryer Grill, I have been successful in making delicious pizzas right inside my kitchen. Well, safe to say my kids just love them! First off, start with baking a pizza bread with the help of the bake function. After that, you can put on the toppings as per your preference and slide it inside the oven! See, easy-breezy!

Reheat

Most of the time, leftover food is dumped in the trash. However, I do not allow that in my house! So, if you cannot figure out what to do with the leftover food, place it inside the PowerXL Air Fryer Grill and enjoy!

The reheat option of PowerXL Air Fryer Grill allows you to heat the leftover food with ease. No matter what type of food it is, this function will not let you waste the food!

Toast

I have always struggled while taking care of multiple cooking appliances in my kitchen. However, with Power XL Air Fryer Grill, I managed to toss out my toaster and made room for other things! With the toast function, you will be able to distribute an equal amount of heat on both sides of a slice of bread. This way, it will turn crispy, making sure you enjoy a great breakfast!

In addition to that, you can also toast bagels with the help of this function. Just cut them into two halves and place them on the wire rack. Select the toast option from the menu and press start.

Accessories

Accessories play an essential role in any type of gadget. It is especially true for an appliance that we use in a kitchen. These assist us in making tasty finger-licking food. Now that you know about Power XL Air Fryer Grill's different functions, let's talk about some of the accessories that come with this appliance.

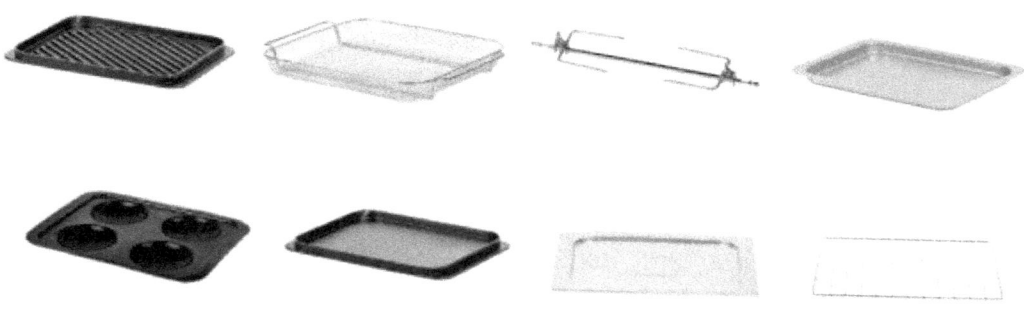

Nonstick Grill Plate

A grill plate will help you make delicious grilled vegetables and other dishes, including chicken and meat. It is made from high-quality aluminium and features a non-stick coating as well. This way, you can cook whatever you want without worrying about the food getting stuck on the plate. Just make sure that you use the required amount of oil to get your dish ready!

Crisper Tray

Another vital accessory that comes with the PowerXL Air Fryer Grill is a crisper tray. Trust me; this one is my favorite! This tray helps you cook food evenly and makes sure that you lead a super healthy life. Yes, you hear me! A crisper tray doesn't require a lot of oil or butter to cook the food. Even after that, the heat gets distributed evenly. Another reason why I love cooking food in a crisper tray!

Rotisserie Spit Set

The rotisserie spit set enables you to cook large pieces of food inside the appliance easily. The setup is quite simple. Firstly, you have to slide the spit rod into the chicken or whatever you are cooking. Then attach this unit with the air fryer grill and press the start button.

The rotisserie spit set will start revolving, and your food will be cooked evenly from all the sides.

Baking Pan

The PowerXL Air Fryer Grill also comes with a baking pan. You can make delicious cookies, cake, and other tasty snacks.

Drip Tray

A drip tray is ideally used when you rotisserie any type of meat, including chicken, lamb, pork, or turkey. It holds the excess fat that drips down from the meat and makes sure that your air fryer grill isn't covered in a mess after the food is all cooked. In addition to that, the drip tray is super easy to clean. Just use a mild dish liquid.

Egg/Muffin Tray

Are you a fan of poached eggs? Well, the PowerXL Air Fryer Grill will make sure you get these in the morning! The egg/muffin tray will enable you to make yummy eggs and muffins. Grease the tray with a cooking spray and crack the egg or pour the batter. Bake it for about seventeen minutes, and you are good to go!

Nonstick Griddle Plate

This cooking device features a flat surface that distributes heat evenly to food when placed inside the PowerXL Air Fryer Grill. Most commonly, it is used to cook pancakes, eggs, sausages, and hash browns.

Oven/Pizza Rack

With the help of an oven/pizza rack, you can cook various food items. From preparing toasts to making yummy pizzas, this super-functional cooking device is truly a savior!

Benefits

Making food in PowerXL Air Fryer Grill is super-duper easy. Moreover, various other things make it one of the best appliances you can use in your kitchen. Keeping that in mind, I have mentioned a few benefits of cooking food with the help of Power XL Air Fryer Grill. I can guarantee you won't regret your decision!

Healthy Food

Our eating habits have turned us obese and unfit. However, if you are trying to bring change in your diet, consuming food with less oil is the trick.

With the help of PowerXL Air Fryer Grill, you minimize the use of oil or butter in your food. Therefore, if you are somebody who loves food and wants to stay fit, PowerXL Air Fryer Grill is a must-have appliance in your kitchen!

Loaded with Accessories

As discussed above, accessories are super essential when it comes to cooking a large amount of food. Therefore, if you buy PowerXL Air Fryer Grill, there is no room for disappointment. There are plenty of accessories which help you make scrumptious food. From desserts to snacks, you can cook anything you like!

8 Cooking Presets

PowerXL Air Fryer Grill comes with eight cooking presets. You can make almost anything using these presets at a very fast speed!

More Superheated Air Flow

The PowerXL Air Fryer Grill makes use of superheated airflow to add more to your favorite meals. It not only makes the food more healthy, but it also makes it crispier and juicer. Besides, you will find the food cooked evenly from all the sides.

Authentic BBQ Flavors & Char Grill Marks

When you use PowerXL Air Fryer Grill to grill your favorite food, the high-density, non-stick grill plate makes sure that it looks authentic. It has raised ridges that create grill marks like any other outdoor BBQ unit. Apart from that, it also infuses the same flavors that you will find at a restaurant. How cool is that!

Chapter 1

Staples

11	Baked Grits
11	Classic Caesar Salad Dressing
12	Asian-Inspired Dipping Sauce
12	Teriyaki Sauce

Baked Grits

Prep time: 3 minutes | Cook time: 1 hour 5 minutes | Makes about 4 cups

- 1 cup grits or polenta (not instant or quick cook)
- 2 cups milk
- 2 cups chicken or vegetable stock
- 2 tablespoons unsalted butter, cut into 4 pieces
- 1 teaspoon kosher salt or ½ teaspoon fine salt

1. Add the grits to the baking pan. Stir in the milk, stock, butter, and salt.
2. Place the pan on the bake position. Select Bake, set the temperature to 325ºF (163ºC), and set the time for 1 hour and 5 minutes.
3. After 15 minutes, remove the pan from the air fryer grill and stir the polenta. Return the pan to the air fryer grill and continue cooking.
4. After 30 minutes, remove the pan again and stir the polenta again. Return the pan to the air fryer grill and continue cooking for 15 to 20 minutes, or until the polenta is soft and creamy and the liquid is absorbed.
5. When done, remove the pan from the air fryer air fryer grill.
6. Serve immediately.

Classic Caesar Salad Dressing

Prep time: 5 minutes | Cook time: 0 minutes | Makes about ⅔ cup

- ½ cup extra-virgin olive oil
- 1 teaspoon anchovy paste
- 2 tablespoons freshly squeezed lemon juice
- ¼ teaspoon kosher salt or ⅛ teaspoon fine salt
- ¼ teaspoon minced or pressed garlic
- 1 egg, beaten

1. Add all the ingredients to a tall, narrow container.
2. Purée the mixture with an immersion blender until smooth.
3. Use immediately.

Asian-Inspired Dipping Sauce

Prep time: 15 minutes | Cook time: 0 minutes | Makes about 1 cup

- 1 tablespoon minced or grated ginger
- 1 tablespoon minced or pressed garlic
- 1 teaspoon chili-garlic sauce or sriracha (or more to taste)
- 3 tablespoons soy sauce
- ¼ cup rice vinegar
- ¼ cup hoisin sauce
- ¼ cup low-sodium chicken or vegetable stock

1. Stir together all the ingredients in a small bowl, or place in a jar with a tight-fitting lid and shake until well mixed.
2. Use immediately.

Teriyaki Sauce

Prep time: 5 minutes | Cook time: 0 minutes | Makes ¾ cup

- ½ cup soy sauce
- 3 tablespoons honey
- 1 tablespoon rice wine or dry sherry
- 1 tablespoon rice vinegar
- 2 teaspoons minced fresh ginger
- 2 garlic cloves, smashed

1. Beat together all the ingredients in a small bowl.
2. Use immediately.

Chapter 2

Breakfasts

15	Bacon Knots
15	Blueberry Tortilla
16	Banana and Carrot Muffin
16	Fresh Berry Pancake
17	Chicken Breast with Apple
17	French Toast Sticks with Strawberry Sauce
18	Apple Pastry
19	Hash Brown Casserole
19	Corned Beef and Eggs Hash
20	Olives, Almond, and Kale Baked Eggs
21	Avocado and Egg Burrito
22	Tomato Omelet with Avocado Dressing

Bacon Knots

Prep time: 5 minutes | Cook time: 7 to 8 minutes | Serves 6

- 1 pound (454 g) maple smoked center-cut bacon
- ¼ cup brown sugar
- ¼ cup maple syrup
- Coarsely cracked black peppercorns, to taste

1. On a clean work surface, tie each bacon strip in a loose knot.
2. Stir together the brown sugar and maple syrup in a bowl. Generously brush this mixture over the bacon knots.
3. Place the bacon knots in the air fryer basket and sprinkle with the coarsely cracked black peppercorns.
4. Place the basket on the bake position. Select Air Fry, set temperature to 390ºF (199ºC), and set time to 8 minutes.
5. After 5 minutes, remove the basket from the air fryer grill and flip the bacon knots. Return the basket to the air fryer grill and continue cooking for 2 to 3 minutes more.
6. When cooking is complete, the bacon should be crisp. Remove from the air fryer grill to a paper towel-lined plate. Let the bacon knots cool for a few minutes and serve warm.

Blueberry Tortilla

Prep time: 5 minutes | Cook time: 4 minutes | Serves 2

- ¼ cup nonfat Ricotta cheese
- ¼ cup plain nonfat Greek yogurt
- 1 tablespoon granulated stevia
- 2 tablespoons finely ground flaxseeds
- ½ teaspoon cinnamon
- ¼ teaspoon vanilla extract
- 2 (8-inch) low-carb whole-wheat tortillas
- ½ cup fresh blueberries, divided

1. Line the sheet pan with the aluminum foil.
2. In a small bowl, whisk together the Ricotta cheese, yogurt, stevia, flaxseeds, cinnamon and vanilla.
3. Place the tortillas on the sheet pan. Spread half of the yogurt mixture on each tortilla, almost to the edges. Top each tortilla with ¼ cup of blueberries. Fold the tortillas in half.
4. Place the pan on the bake position.
5. Select Bake, set temperature to 400ºF (205ºC) and set time to 4 minutes.
6. When cooking is complete, remove the pan from the air fryer grill. Serve immediately.

Banana and Carrot Muffin

Prep time: 10 minutes | Cook time: 20 minutes | Serves 12

- 1½ cups whole-wheat flour
- 1 cup grated carrot
- 1 cup mashed banana
- ½ cup bran
- ½ cup low-fat buttermilk
- 2 tablespoons agave nectar
- 2 teaspoons baking powder
- 1 teaspoon vanilla
- 1 teaspoon baking soda
- ½ teaspoon nutmeg
- Pinch cloves
- 2 egg whites

1. Line a muffin pan with 12 paper liners.
2. In a large bowl, stir together all the ingredients. Mix well, but do not over beat.
3. Scoop the mixture into the muffin cups.
4. Place the pan on the bake position.
5. Select Bake, set temperature to 400ºF (205ºC) and set time to 20 minutes.
6. When cooking is complete, remove the pan and let rest for 5 minutes.
7. Serve warm or at room temperature.

Fresh Berry Pancake

Prep time: 10 minutes | Cook time: 14 minutes | Serves 4

- 1 tablespoon unsalted butter, at room temperature
- 1 egg
- 2 egg whites
- ½ cup whole-wheat pastry flour
- ½ cup 2% milk
- 1 teaspoon pure vanilla extract
- 1 cup sliced fresh strawberries
- ½ cup fresh blueberries
- ½ cup fresh raspberries

1. Grease a baking pan with the butter.
2. Using a hand mixer, beat together the egg, egg whites, pastry flour, milk, and vanilla in a medium mixing bowl until well incorporated.
3. Pour the batter into the pan.
4. Place the pan on the bake position.
5. Select Bake, set temperature to 330ºF (166ºC) and set time to 14 minutes.
6. When cooked, the pancake should puff up in the center and the edges should be golden brown
7. Allow the pancake to cool for 5 minutes and serve topped with the berries.

Chicken Breast with Apple

Prep time: 15 minutes | Cook time: 10 minutes | Makes 8 patties

- 1 egg white
- 2 garlic cloves, minced
- 1 Granny Smith apple, peeled and finely chopped
- 1/3 cup minced onion
- 3 tablespoons ground almonds
- 2 tablespoons apple juice
- 1/8 teaspoon freshly ground black pepper
- 1 pound (454 g) ground chicken breast

1. Combine all the ingredients except the chicken in a medium mixing bowl and stir well.
2. Add the chicken breast to the apple mixture and mix with your hands until well incorporated.
3. Divide the mixture into 8 equal portions and shape into patties. Arrange the patties in the air fry basket.
4. Place the air fry basket on the air fry position.
5. Select Air Fry, set temperature to 330ºF (166ºC) and set time to 10 minutes.
6. When done, a meat thermometer inserted in the center of the chicken should reach at least 165ºF (74ºC).
7. Remove from the air fryer grill to a plate. Let the chicken cool for 5 minutes and serve warm.

French Toast Sticks with Strawberry Sauce

Prep time: 5 minutes | Cook time: 12 minutes | Serves 4

- 3 slices low-sodium whole-wheat bread, each cut into 4 strips
- 1 tablespoon unsalted butter, melted
- 1 tablespoon sugar
- 1 tablespoon 2 percent milk
- 1 egg, beaten
- 1 egg white
- 1 cup sliced fresh strawberries
- 1 tablespoon freshly squeezed lemon juice

1. Arrange the bread strips on a plate and drizzle with the melted butter.
2. In a bowl, whisk together the sugar, milk, egg and egg white.
3. Dredge the bread strips into the egg mixture and place on a wire rack to let the batter drip off. Arrange half the coated bread strips on the sheet pan.
4. Place the pan on the air fry position.

Breakfasts |17

5. Select Air Fry, set temperature to 380ºF (193ºC) and set time to 6 minutes.
6. After 3 minutes, remove the pan from the air fryer grill. Use tongs to turn the strips over. Rotate the pan and return the pan to the air fryer grill to continue cooking.
7. When cooking is complete, the strips should be golden brown.
8. In a small bowl, mash the strawberries with a fork and stir in the lemon juice. Serve the French toast sticks with the strawberry sauce.

Apple Pastry

Prep time: 10 minutes | Cook time: 20 minutes | Serves 4

- 1 cup diced apple
- 1 tablespoon brown sugar
- 1 teaspoon freshly squeezed lemon juice
- 1 teaspoon all-purpose flour, plus more for dusting
- ¼ teaspoon cinnamon
- ⅛ teaspoon allspice
- ½ package frozen puff pastry, thawed
- 1 large egg, beaten
- 2 teaspoons granulated sugar

1. Whisk together the apple, lemon juice, brown sugar, flour, cinnamon and allspice in a medium bowl.
2. On a clean work surface, lightly dust with the flour and lay the puff pastry sheet. Using a rolling pin, gently roll the dough to smooth out the folds, seal any tears and form it into a square. Cut the dough into four squares.
3. Spoon a quarter of the apple mixture into the center of each puff pastry square and spread it evenly in a triangle shape over half the pastry, leaving a border of about ½ inch around the edges of the pastry. Fold the pastry diagonally over the filling to form triangles. With a fork, crimp the edges to seal them. Place the turnovers on the sheet pan, spacing them evenly.
4. Cut two or three small slits in the top of each turnover. Brush with the egg. Sprinkle evenly with the granulated sugar.
5. Place the pan on the bake position.
6. Select Bake, set temperature to 350ºF (180ºC) and set time to 20 minutes.
7. After 10 to 12 minutes, remove the pan from the air fryer grill. Check the pastries. If they are browned unevenly, rotate the pan. Return the pan to the air fryer grill and continue cooking.
8. When cooking is complete, remove the pan from the air fryer grill. The turnovers should be golden brown and the filling bubbling. Let cool for about 10 minutes before serving.

Hash Brown Casserole

Prep time: 15 minutes | Cook time: 30 minutes | Serves 4

- 3½ cups frozen hash browns, thawed
- 1 teaspoon salt
- 1 teaspoon freshly ground black pepper
- 1 (10.5-ounce / 298-g) can cream of chicken soup
- 3 tablespoons butter, melted
- ½ cup sour cream
- 1 cup minced onion
- ½ cup shredded sharp Cheddar cheese
- Cooking spray

1. Put the hash browns in a large bowl and season with salt and black pepper. Add the cream of chicken soup, melted butter, and sour cream and stir until well incorporated. Mix in the minced onion and cheese and stir well.
2. Spray a baking pan with cooking spray.
3. Spread the hash brown mixture evenly into the baking pan.
4. Place the pan on the bake position.
5. Select Bake, set temperature to 325ºF (163ºC) and set time to 30 minutes.
6. When cooked, the hash brown mixture will be browned.
7. Cool for 5 minutes before serving.

Corned Beef and Eggs Hash

Prep time: 10 minutes | Cook time: 25 minutes | Serves 4

- 2 medium Yukon Gold potatoes, peeled and cut into ¼-inch cubes
- 1 medium onion, chopped
- ⅓ cup diced red bell pepper
- 3 tablespoons vegetable oil
- ½ teaspoon kosher salt, divided
- ½ teaspoon freshly ground black pepper, divided
- ½ teaspoon dried thyme
- ¾ pound (340 g) corned beef, cut into ¼-inch pieces
- 4 large eggs

1. In a large bowl, stir together the potatoes, onion, red pepper, vegetable oil, ¼ teaspoon of the salt, ¼ teaspoon of the pepper and thyme. Spread the vegetable mixture on the sheet pan in an even layer.
2. Place the pan on the toast position.
3. Select Toast, set temperature to 375ºF (190ºC) and set time to 25 minutes.

Breakfasts | 19

4. After 15 minutes, remove the pan from the air fryer grill and add the corned beef. Stir the mixture to incorporate the corned beef. Return the pan to the air fryer grill and continue cooking.
5. After 5 minutes, remove the pan from the air fryer grill. Using a large spoon, create 4 circles in the hash to hold the eggs. Gently crack an egg into each circle. Season the eggs with the remaining ¼ teaspoon of the salt and ¼ teaspoon of the pepper. Return the pan to the air fryer grill. Continue cooking for 3 to 5 minutes, depending on how you like your eggs.
6. When cooking is complete, remove the pan from the air fryer grill. Serve immediately.

Olives, Almond, and Kale Baked Eggs

Prep time: 5 minutes | Cook time: 11 minutes | Serves 2

- 1 cup roughly chopped kale leaves, stems and center ribs removed
- ¼ cup grated pecorino cheese
- ¼ cup olive oil
- 3 tablespoons whole almonds
- 1 garlic clove, peeled
- Kosher salt and freshly ground black pepper, to taste
- 4 large eggs
- 2 tablespoons heavy cream
- 3 tablespoons chopped pitted mixed olives

1. Place the kale, pecorino, olive oil, almonds, garlic, salt, and pepper in a small blender and blitz until well incorporated.
2. One at a time, crack the eggs in a baking pan. Drizzle the kale pesto on top of the egg whites. Top the yolks with the cream and swirl together the yolks and the pesto.
3. Place the pan on the bake position.
4. Select Bake, set temperature to 300ºF (150ºC) and set time to 11 minutes.
5. When cooked, the top should begin to brown and the eggs should be set.
6. Allow the eggs to cool for 5 minutes. Scatter the olives on top and serve warm.

Avocado and Egg Burrito

Prep time: 10 minutes | Cook time: 4 minutes | Serves 4

- 4 low-sodium whole-wheat flour tortillas

Filling:
- 1 hard-boiled egg, chopped
- 2 hard-boiled egg whites, chopped
- 1 red bell pepper, chopped
- 1 ripe avocado, peeled, pitted, and chopped
- 1 (1.2-ounce / 34-g) slice low-sodium, low-fat American cheese, torn into pieces
- 3 tablespoons low-sodium salsa, plus additional for serving (optional)

Special Equipment:
- 4 toothpicks (optional), soaked in water for at least 30 minutes

1. Make the filling: Combine the egg, egg whites, red bell pepper, avocado, cheese, and salsa in a medium bowl and stir until blended.
2. Assemble the burritos: Arrange the tortillas on a clean work surface and place ¼ of the prepared filling in the middle of each tortilla, leaving about 1½-inch on each end unfilled. Fold in the opposite sides of each tortilla and roll up. Secure with toothpicks through the center, if needed.
3. Transfer the burritos to the air fry basket.
4. Place the air fry basket on the air fry position.
5. Select Air Fry, set temperature to 390ºF (199ºC) and set time to 4 minutes.
6. When cooking is complete, the burritos should be crisp and golden brown.
7. Allow to cool for 5 minutes and serve with salsa, if desired.

Tomato Omelet with Avocado Dressing

Prep time: 10 minutes | Cook time: 20 minutes | Serves 2 or 3

- ½ cup cherry tomatoes, halved
- Kosher salt, to taste
- 6 large eggs, lightly beaten
- ½ cup fresh corn kernels
- ¼ cup milk
- 1 tablespoon finely chopped fresh dill
- Freshly ground black pepper, to taste
- ½ cup shredded Monterey Jack cheese

Avocado Dressing:
- 1 ripe avocado, pitted and peeled
- ¼ cup olive oil
- 2 tablespoons fresh lime juice
- 8 fresh basil leaves, finely chopped
- 1 scallion, finely chopped

1. Put the tomato halves in a colander and lightly season with salt. Set aside for 10 minutes to drain well. Pour the tomatoes into a large bowl and fold in the eggs, corn, milk, and dill. Sprinkle with salt and pepper and stir until mixed.
2. Pour the egg mixture into a baking pan.
3. Place the pan on the bake position.
4. Select Bake, set temperature to 300ºF (150ºC) and set time to 15 minutes.
5. When done, remove the pan from the air fryer grill. Scatter the cheese on top.
6. Select Bake, set temperature to 315ºF (157ºC) and set time to 5 minutes. Return the pan to the air fryer grill.
7. Meanwhile, make the avocado dressing: Mash the avocado with the lime juice in a medium bowl until smooth. Mix in the olive oil, scallion, and basil and stir until well incorporated.
8. When cooking is complete, the frittata will be puffy and set. Let the frittata cool for 5 minutes and serve alongside the avocado dressing.

Chapter 3

Fish and Seafood

- 25 Fruity Sweet-Sour Snapper Fillet
- 25 Spiced Red Snapper Fillet
- 26 Gold Salmon Patties
- 26 Pecan-Crusted Catfish
- 27 Southern Salmon Bowl
- 27 Butter-Wine Baked Salmon Steak
- 28 Crispy Halibut Fillets
- 28 Tuna Patties with Cheese Sauced
- 29 Snapper Fillets
- 30 Hoisin Tuna with Jasmine Rice
- 30 Breaded Crab Sticks with Mayo Sauce
- 31 Toasted Scallops with Mushrooms

Fruity Sweet-Sour Snapper Fillet

Prep time: 15 minutes | Cook time: 12 minutes | Serves 4

- 4 (4-ounce / 113-g) red snapper fillets
- 2 teaspoons olive oil
- 3 plums, halved and pitted
- 3 nectarines, halved and pitted
- 1 cup red grapes
- 1 tablespoon freshly squeezed lemon juice
- 1 tablespoon honey
- ½ teaspoon dried thyme

1. Arrange the red snapper fillets in the air fry basket and drizzle the olive oil over the top.
2. Place the basket on the air fry position.
3. Select Air Fry, set temperature to 390ºF (199ºC), and set time to 12 minutes.
4. After 4 minutes, remove the basket from the air fryer grill. Top the fillets with the plums and nectarines. Scatter the red grapes all over the fillets. Drizzle with the honey and lemon juice and sprinkle the thyme on top. Return the basket to the air fryer grill and continue cooking for 8 minutes, or until the fish is flaky.
5. When cooking is complete, remove from the air fryer grill and serve warm.

Spiced Red Snapper Fillet

Prep time: 13 minutes | Cook time: 10 minutes | Serves 4

- 1 teaspoon olive oil
- 1½ teaspoons black pepper
- ¼ teaspoon garlic powder
- ¼ teaspoon thyme
- ⅛ teaspoon cayenne pepper
- 4 (4-ounce / 113-g) red snapper fillets, skin on
- 4 thin slices lemon
- Nonstick cooking spray

1. Spritz the air fry basket with nonstick cooking spray.
2. In a small bowl, stir together the olive oil, black pepper, thyme, garlic powder, and cayenne pepper. Rub the mixture all over the fillets until completely coated.
3. Lay the fillets, skin-side down, in the air fry basket and top each fillet with a slice of lemon.
4. Place the basket on the bake position.
5. Select Bake, set temperature to 390ºF (199ºC), and set time to 10 minutes. Flip the fillets halfway through.
6. When cooking is complete, the fish should be cooked through. Let the fish cool for 5 minutes and serve.

Gold Salmon Patties

Prep time: 5 minutes | Cook time: 11 minutes | Makes 6 patties

- 1 (14.75-ounce / 418-g) can Alaskan pink salmon, drained and bones removed
- ½ cup bread crumbs
- 1 egg, whisked
- 2 scallions, diced
- 1 teaspoon garlic powder
- Salt and pepper, to taste
- Cooking spray

1. Stir together the salmon, bread crumbs, whisked egg, garlic powder, scallions, salt, and pepper in a large bowl until well incorporated.
2. Divide the salmon mixture into six equal portions and form each into a patty with your hands.
3. Arrange the salmon patties in the air fry basket and spritz them with cooking spray.
4. Place the basket on the air fry position.
5. Air Fry, set temperature to 400ºF (205ºC), and set time to 10 minutes. Flip the patties once halfway through.
6. When cooking is complete, the patties should be golden brown and cooked through. Remove the patties from the air fryer grill and serve on a plate.

Pecan-Crusted Catfish

Prep time: 5 minutes | Cook time: 12 minutes | Serves 4

- ½ cup pecan meal
- 1 teaspoon fine sea salt
- ¼ teaspoon ground black pepper

For Garnish (Optional):
- Fresh oregano
- 4 (4-ounce / 113-g) catfish fillets
- Avocado oil spray
- Pecan halves

1. Spray the air fry basket with avocado oil spray.
2. Combine the sea salt, black pepper and pecan meal in a large bowl. Dredge each catfish fillet in the meal mixture, turning until well coated. Spritz the fillets with avocado oil spray, then transfer to the air fry basket.
3. Place the basket on the air fry position.
4. Select Air Fry, set temperature to 375ºF (190ºC), and set time to 12 minutes. Flip the fillets halfway through the cooking time.
5. When cooking is complete, the fish should be cooked through and no longer translucent. Remove from the air fryer grill and sprinkle the oregano sprigs and pecan halves on top for garnish, if desired. Serve immediately.

Southern Salmon Bowl

Prep time: 115 minutes | Cook time: 12 minutes | Serves 4

- 12 ounces (340 g) salmon fillets, cut into 1½-inch cubes
- 1 red onion, chopped
- 1 jalapeño pepper, minced
- 1 red bell pepper, chopped
- ¼ cup low-sodium salsa
- 2 teaspoons peanut oil or safflower oil
- 2 tablespoons low-sodium tomato juice
- 1 teaspoon chili powder

1. Mix together the salmon cubes, red onion, red bell pepper, jalapeño, peanut oil, tomato juice, salsa, chili powder in a medium metal bowl and stir until well incorporated.
2. Place the metal bowl on the bake position.
3. Select Bake, set temperature to 370°F (188°C), and set time to 12 minutes. Stir the ingredients once halfway through the cooking time.
4. When cooking is complete, the salmon should be cooked through and the veggies should be fork-tender. Serve warm.

Butter-Wine Baked Salmon Steak

Prep time: 5 minutes | Cook time: 10 minutes | Serves 4

- 4 tablespoons butter, melted
- 2 cloves garlic, minced
- Sea salt and ground black pepper, to taste
- ¼ cup dry white wine
- 1 tablespoon lime juice
- 1 teaspoon smoked paprika
- ½ teaspoon onion powder
- 4 salmon steaks
- Cooking spray

1. Place all the ingredients except the salmon and oil in a shallow dish and stir to mix well.
2. Add the salmon steaks, turning to coat well on both sides. Transfer the salmon to the refrigerator to marinate for 30 minutes.
3. When ready, put the salmon steaks in the air fry basket, discarding any excess marinade. Spray the salmon steaks with cooking spray.
4. Place the basket on the air fry position.
5. Select Air Fry, set temperature to 360°F (182°C), and set time to 10 minutes. Flip the salmon steaks halfway through.
6. When cooking is complete, remove from the air fryer grill and divide the salmon steaks among four plates. Serve warm.

Crispy Halibut Fillets

Prep time: 5 minutes | Cook time: 10 minutes | Serves 4

- 2 medium-sized halibut fillets
- Dash of tabasco sauce
- 1 teaspoon curry powder
- ½ teaspoon ground coriander
- ½ teaspoon hot paprika
- Kosher salt and freshly cracked mixed peppercorns, to taste
- 2 eggs
- ½ cup grated Parmesan cheese
- 1½ tablespoons olive oil

1. On a clean work surface, drizzle the halibut fillets with the tabasco sauce. Sprinkle with the curry powder, hot paprika, coriander, salt, and cracked mixed peppercorns. Set aside.
2. In a shallow bowl, beat the eggs until frothy. In another shallow bowl, combine the Parmesan cheese and olive oil.
3. One at a time, dredge the halibut fillets in the beaten eggs, shaking off any excess, then roll them over the Parmesan cheese until evenly coated.
4. Arrange the halibut fillets in the air fry basket in a single layer.
5. Place the basket on the toast position.
6. Select Toast, set temperature to 365ºF (185ºC), and set time to 10 minutes.
7. When cooking is complete, the fish should be golden brown and crisp. Cool for 5 minutes before serving.

Tuna Patties with Cheese Sauced

Prep time: 5 minutes | Cook time: 17 to 18 minutes | Serves 4

Tuna Patties:
- 1 pound (454 g) canned tuna, drained
- 1 egg, whisked
- 2 tablespoons shallots, minced
- 1 garlic clove, minced

Cheese Sauce:
- 1 tablespoon butter
- 1 cup beer
- 1 cup grated Romano cheese
- Sea salt and ground black pepper, to taste
- 1 tablespoon sesame oil
- 2 tablespoons grated Colby cheese

1. Mix together the canned tuna, whisked egg, cheese, shallots, salt, and pepper in a large bowl and stir to incorporate.
2. Divide the tuna mixture into four equal portions and form each portion into a patty with your hands. Refrigerate the patties for 2 hours.

3. When ready, brush both sides of each patty with sesame oil, then place in the air fry basket.
4. Place the basket on the bake position.
5. Select Bake, set temperature to 360ºF (182ºC), and set time to 14 minutes. Flip the patties halfway through the cooking time.
6. Meanwhile, melt the butter in a saucepan over medium heat.
7. Pour in the beer and whisk constantly, or until it begins to bubble. Add the grated Colby cheese and mix well. Continue cooking for 3 to 4 minutes, or until the cheese melts. Remove from the heat.
8. When cooking is complete, the patties should be lightly browned and cooked through. Remove the patties from the air fryer grill to a plate. Drizzle them with the cheese sauce and serve immediately.

Snapper Fillets

Prep time: 9 minutes | Cook time: 18 minutes | Serves 4

- 2 tablespoons extra-virgin olive oil
- 2 large garlic cloves, minced
- ½ onion, finely chopped
- 1 (14.5-ounce / 411-g) can diced tomatoes, drained
- ¼ cup sliced green olives
- 3 tablespoons capers, divided
- 2 tablespoons chopped fresh parsley, divided
- ½ teaspoon dried oregano
- 4 (6-ounce / 170-g) snapper fillets
- ½ teaspoon kosher salt

1. Grease the sheet pan generously with olive oil, then place the pan on the toast position.
2. Select Toast, set temperature to 375ºF (190ºC), and set time to 18 minutes. Select
3. Remove the pan and add the garlic and onion to the olive oil in the pan, stirring to coat. Return the pan to the air fryer grill and continue cooking.
4. After 2 minutes, remove the pan from the air fryer grill. Stir in the olives, tomatoes, 1½ tablespoons of capers, 1 tablespoon of parsley, and oregano. Return the pan to the air fryer grill and continue cooking for 6 minutes until heated through.
5. Meanwhile, rub the fillets with the salt on both sides.
6. After another 6 minutes, remove the pan. Put the fillets in the center of the sheet pan and spoon some of the sauce over them. Return the pan to the air fryer grill and continue cooking, or until the fish is flaky.
7. When cooked, remove the pan from the air fryer grill. Scatter the remaining 1 tablespoon of parsley of capers and 1½ tablespoons on top of the fillets, then serve.

Fish and Seafood

Hoisin Tuna with Jasmine Rice

Prep time: 15 minutes | Cook time: 5 minutes | Serves 4

- ½ cup hoisin sauce
- 2 tablespoons rice wine vinegar
- 2 teaspoons sesame oil
- 2 teaspoons dried lemongrass
- 1 teaspoon garlic powder
- ¼ teaspoon red pepper flakes
- ½ small onion, quartered and thinly sliced
- 8 ounces (227 g) fresh tuna, cut into 1-inch cubes
- Cooking spray
- 3 cups cooked jasmine rice

1. In a small bowl, whisk together the vinegar, hoisin sauce, sesame oil, garlic powder, lemongrass, and red pepper flakes.
2. Add the sliced onion and tuna cubes and gently toss until the fish is evenly coated.
3. Arrange the coated tuna cubes in the air fry basket in a single layer.
4. Place the basket on the air fry position.
5. Select Air Fry, set temperature to 390ºF (199ºC), and set time to 5 minutes. Flip the fish halfway through the cooking time.
6. When cooking is complete, the fish should begin to flake. Continue cooking for 1 minute, if necessary. Remove from the air fryer grill and serve over hot jasmine rice.

Breaded Crab Sticks with Mayo Sauce

Prep time: 5 minutes | Cook time: 12 minutes | Serves 4

Crab Sticks:
- 2 eggs
- 1 cup flour
- 1/3 cup panko bread crumbs

Mayo Sauce:
- ½ cup mayonnaise
- 1 lime, juiced
- 1 tablespoon old bay seasoning
- 1 pound (454 g) crab sticks
- Cooking spray
- 2 garlic cloves, minced

1. In a bowl, beat the eggs. In a shallow bowl, place the flour. In another shallow bowl, thoroughly combine the panko bread crumbs and old bay seasoning.
2. Dredge the crab sticks in the flour, shaking off any excess, then in the beaten eggs, finally press them in the bread crumb mixture to coat well.
3. Arrange the crab sticks in the air fry basket and spray with cooking spray.
4. Place the basket on the air fry position.

5. Select Air Fry, set temperature to 390ºF (199ºC), and set time to 12 minutes. Flip the crab sticks halfway through the cooking time.
6. Meanwhile, make the sauce by whisking together the mayo, lime juice, and garlic in a small bowl.
7. When cooking is complete, remove the basket from the air fryer grill. Serve the crab sticks with the mayo sauce on the side.

Toasted Scallops with Mushrooms

Prep time: 10 minutes | Cook time: 8 minutes | Serves 4

- 1 pound (454 g) sea scallops
- 3 tablespoons hoisin sauce
- ½ cup toasted sesame seeds
- 6 ounces (170 g) snow peas, trimmed
- 3 teaspoons vegetable oil, divided
- 1 teaspoon soy sauce
- 1 teaspoon sesame oil
- 1 cup Toasted mushrooms

1. Brush the scallops with the hoisin sauce. Put the sesame seeds in a shallow dish. Roll the scallops in the sesame seeds until evenly coated.
2. Combine the snow peas with the sesame oil, 1 teaspoon of vegetable oil, and soy sauce in a medium bowl and toss to coat.
3. Grease the sheet pan with the remaining 2 teaspoons of vegetable oil. Put the scallops in the middle of the pan and arrange the snow peas around the scallops in a single layer.
4. Place the pan on the toast position.
5. Select Toast, set temperature to 375ºF (190ºC), and set time to 8 minutes.
6. After 5 minutes, remove the pan and flip the scallops. Fold in the mushrooms and stir well. Return the pan to the air fryer grill and continue cooking.
7. When done, remove the pan from the air fryer grill and cool for 5 minutes. Serve warm.

Chapter 4

Meats

34	Authentic Carne Asada
34	London Broil with Peanut Dipping Sauce
35	Sweet-Sour London Broil
36	Breaded Calf's Liver Strips
36	Schnitzels with Sour Cream and Dill Sauce
37	Garlicky Veal Loin
38	Macadamia Nuts Breaded Pork Rack
38	Honey New York Strip
39	Ground Beef and Spinach Meatloaves
40	Tangy Pork Ribs
40	Smoked Paprika Pork and Vegetable Kabobs
41	Char Siu (Chinese BBQ Pork)

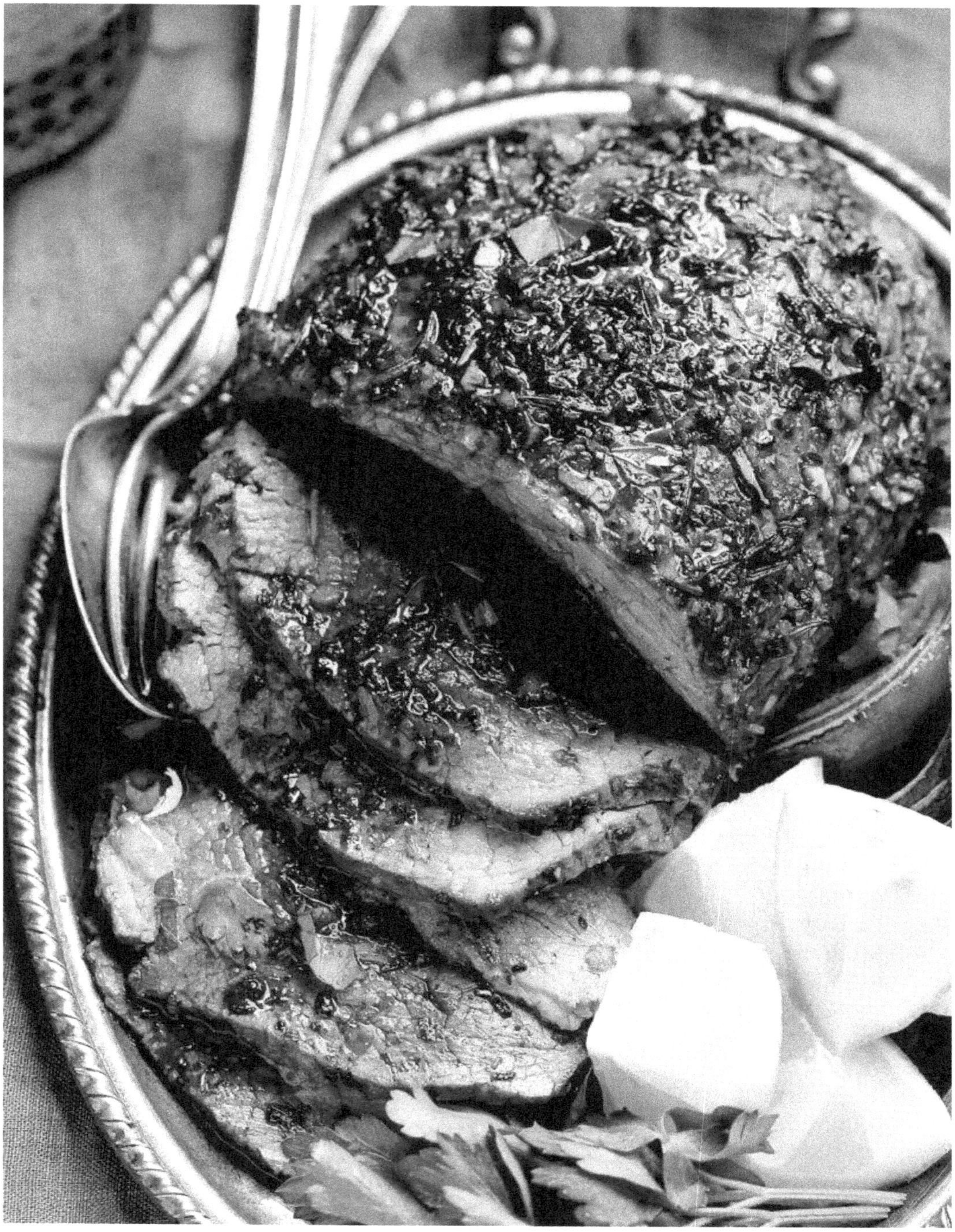

Authentic Carne Asada

Prep time: 5 minutes | Cook time: 15 minutes | Serves 4

- 3 chipotle peppers in adobo, chopped
- ⅓ cup chopped fresh oregano
- ⅓ cup chopped fresh parsley
- 4 cloves garlic, minced
- Juice of 2 limes
- 1 teaspoon ground cumin seeds
- ⅓ cup olive oil
- 1 to 1½ pounds (454 g to 680 g) flank steak
- Salt, to taste

1. Combine the oregano, garlic, chipotle, parsley, cumin, lime juice, and olive oil in a large bowl. Stir to mix well.
2. Dunk the flank steak in the mixture and press to coat well. Wrap the bowl in plastic and marinate under room temperature for at least 30 minutes.
3. Discard the marinade and place the steak in the air fry basket. Sprinkle with salt.
4. Place the basket on the air fry position.
5. Select Air Fry. Set temperature to 390ºF (199ºC) and set time to 15 minutes. Flip the steak halfway through the cooking time.
6. When cooking is complete, the steak should be medium-rare or reach your desired doneness.
7. Remove the steak from the air fryer grill and slice to serve.

London Broil with Peanut Dipping Sauce

Prep time: 30 minutes | Cook time: 5 minutes | Serves 4

- 8 ounces (227 g) London broil, sliced into 8 strips
- 2 teaspoons curry powder

Peanut Dipping sauce:
- 2 tablespoons creamy peanut butter
- 1 tablespoon reduced-sodium soy sauce
- ½ teaspoon kosher salt
- Cooking spray

- 2 teaspoons rice vinegar
- 1 teaspoon honey
- 1 teaspoon grated ginger

Special Equipment:
- 4 bamboo skewers, cut into halves and soaked in water for 20 minutes to keep them from burning while cooking

1. Spritz the air fry basket with cooking spray.
2. In a bowl, place the London broil strips and sprinkle with the curry powder and kosher salt to season. Thread the strips onto the soaked skewers.
3. Arrange the skewers in the prepared basket and spritz with cooking spray.
4. Place the basket on the air fry position.
5. Select Air Fry. Set temperature to 360ºF (182ºC) and set time to 5 minutes. Flip the beef halfway through the cooking time.
6. When cooking is complete, the beef should be well browned.
7. In the meantime, stir together the soy sauce, honey, peanut butter, rice vinegar, and ginger in a bowl to make the dipping sauce.
8. Transfer the beef to the serving dishes and let rest for 5 minutes. Serve with the peanut dipping sauce on the side.

Sweet-Sour London Broil

Prep time: 8 hours 5 minutes | Cook time: 25 minutes | Serves 6

- 2 tablespoons Worcestershire sauce
- 2 tablespoons minced onion
- ¼ cup honey
- ⅔ cup ketchup
- 2 tablespoons apple cider vinegar
- ½ teaspoon paprika
- ¼ cup olive oil
- 1 teaspoon salt
- 1 teaspoon freshly ground black pepper
- 2 pounds (907 g) London broil, top round (about 1-inch thick)

1. Combine all the ingredients, except for the London broil, in a large bowl. Stir to mix well.
2. Pierce the meat with a fork generously on both sides, then dunk the meat in the mixture and press to coat well.
3. Wrap the bowl in plastic and refrigerate to marinate for at least 8 hours.
4. Discard the marinade and transfer the London broil to the air fry basket.
5. Place the basket on the air fry position.
6. Select Air Fry. Set temperature to 400ºF (205ºC) and set time to 25 minutes. Flip the meat halfway through the cooking time.
7. When cooking is complete, the meat should be well browned.
8. Transfer the cooked London broil on a plate and allow to cool for 5 minutes before slicing to serve.

Breaded Calf's Liver Strips

Prep time: 15 minutes | Cook time: 5 minutes | Serves 4

- 1 pound (454 g) sliced calf's liver, cut into ½-inch wide strips
- 2 eggs
- 2 tablespoons milk
- ½ cup whole wheat flour
- 2 cups panko bread crumbs
- Salt and ground black pepper, to taste
- Cooking spray

1. Spritz the air fry basket with cooking spray.
2. Rub the calf's liver strips with ground black pepper and salt on a clean work surface.
3. Whisk the eggs with milk in a large bowl. Pour the flour in a shallow dish. Pour the panko on a separate shallow dish.
4. Dunk the liver strips in the flour, then in the egg mixture. Shake the excess off and roll the strips over the panko to coat well.
5. Arrange the liver strips in the basket and spritz with cooking spray.
6. Place the basket on the air fry position.
7. Select Air Fry. Set temperature to 390ºF (199ºC) and set time to 5 minutes. Flip the strips halfway through.
8. When cooking is complete, the strips should be browned.
9. Serve immediately.

Schnitzels with Sour Cream and Dill Sauce

Prep time: 5 minutes | Cook time: 4 minutes | Serves 4 to 6

- ½ cup flour
- 1½ teaspoons salt
- Freshly ground black pepper, to taste
- 2 eggs
- ½ cup milk
- 1½ cups toasted bread crumbs
- 1 teaspoon paprika
- 6 boneless, center cut pork chops (about 1½ pounds / 680 g), fat trimmed, pound to ½-inch thick
- 2 tablespoons olive oil
- 3 tablespoons melted butter
- Lemon wedges, for serving
- Sour Cream and Dill Sauce:
- 1 cup chicken stock
- 1½ tablespoons cornstarch
- ⅓ cup sour cream
- 1½ tablespoons chopped fresh dill
- Salt and ground black pepper, to taste

1. Combine the flour with salt and black pepper in a large bowl. Stir to mix well. Whisk the egg with milk in a second bowl. Stir the bread crumbs and paprika in a third bowl.

2. Dredge the pork chops in the flour bowl, then in the egg milk, and then into the bread crumbs bowl. Press to coat well. Shake the excess off.
3. Arrange the pork chop in the air fry basket, then brush with olive oil and butter on all sides.
4. Place the basket on the air fry position.
5. Select Air Fry. Set temperature to 400ºF (205ºC) and set time to 4 minutes.
6. After 2 minutes, remove the basket from the air fryer grill. Flip the pork. Return the basket to the air fryer grill and continue cooking.
7. When cooking is complete, the pork chop should be golden brown and crispy.
8. Meanwhile, combine the chicken stock and cornstarch in a small saucepan and bring to a boil over medium-high heat. Simmer for 2 more minutes.
9. Turn off the heat, then mix in the fresh dill, sour cream, salt, and black pepper.
10. Remove the schnitzels from the air fryer grill to a plate and baste with sour cream and dill sauce. Squeeze the lemon wedges over and slice to serve.

Garlicky Veal Loin

Prep time: 1 hour 10 minutes | Cook time: 12 minutes | Makes 3 veal chops

- 1½ teaspoons crushed fennel seeds
- 1 tablespoon minced fresh rosemary leaves
- 1 tablespoon minced garlic
- 1½ teaspoons lemon zest
- 1½ teaspoons salt
- ½ teaspoon red pepper flakes
- 2 tablespoons olive oil
- 3 (10-ounce / 284-g) bone-in veal loin, about ½ inch thick

1. Combine all the ingredients, except for the veal loin, in a large bowl. Stir to mix well.
2. Dunk the loin in the mixture and press to submerge. Wrap the bowl in plastic and refrigerate for at least an hour to marinate.
3. Arrange the veal loin in the air fry basket.
4. Place the basket on the air fry position.
5. Select Air Fry. Set temperature to 400ºF (205ºC) and set time to 12 minutes. Flip the veal halfway through.
6. When cooking is complete, the internal temperature of the veal should reach at least 145ºF (63ºC) for medium rare.
7. Serve immediately.

Macadamia Nuts Breaded Pork Rack

Prep time: 5 minutes | Cook time: 35 minutes | Serves 2

- 1 clove garlic, minced
- 2 tablespoons olive oil
- 1 pound (454 g) rack of pork
- 1 cup chopped macadamia nuts
- 1 tablespoon bread crumbs
- 1 tablespoon rosemary, chopped
- 1 egg
- Salt and ground black pepper, to taste

1. Combine the garlic and olive oil in a small bowl. Stir to mix well.
2. On a clean work surface, rub the pork rack with the sprinkle and garlic oil with salt and black pepper on both sides.
3. Combine the macadamia nuts, bread crumbs, and rosemary in a shallow dish. Whisk the egg in a large bowl.
4. Dredge the pork in the egg, then roll the pork over the macadamia nut mixture to coat well. Shake the excess off.
5. Arrange the pork in the air fry basket.
6. Place the basket on the air fry position.
7. Select Air Fry. Set temperature to 350ºF (180ºC) and set time to 30 minutes.
8. After 30 minutes, remove the basket from the air fryer grill. Flip the pork rack. Return the basket to the air fryer grill and increase temperature to 390ºF (199ºC) and set time to 5 minutes. Keep cooking.
9. When cooking is complete, the pork should be browned.
10. Serve immediately.

Honey New York Strip

Prep time: 5 minutes | Cook time: 14 minutes | Serves 4

- 2 pounds (907 g) New York Strip
- 1 teaspoon cayenne pepper
- 1 tablespoon honey
- 1 tablespoon Dijon mustard
- ½ stick butter, softened
- Sea salt and freshly ground black pepper, to taste
- Cooking spray

1. Spritz the air fry basket with cooking spray.
2. Sprinkle the New York Strip with salt, cayenne pepper, and black pepper on a clean work surface.
3. Arrange the New York Strip in the prepared basket and spritz with cooking spray.
4. Place the basket on the air fry position.

5. Select Air Fry. Set temperature to 400°F (205°C) and set time to 14 minutes. Flip the New York Strip halfway through.
6. When cooking is complete, the strips should be browned.
7. Meanwhile, combine the mustard, honey, and butter in a small bowl. Stir to mix well.
8. Transfer the air fried New York Strip onto a plate and baste with the honey-mustard butter before serving.

Ground Beef and Spinach Meatloaves

Prep time: 15 minutes | Cook time: 45 minutes | Serves 2

- 1 large egg, beaten
- 1 cup frozen spinach
- 1/3 cup almond meal
- ¼ cup chopped onion
- ¼ cup plain Greek milk
- ¼ teaspoon salt
- ¼ teaspoon dried sage
- 2 teaspoons olive oil, divided
- Freshly ground black pepper, to taste
- ½ pound (227 g) extra-lean ground beef
- ¼ cup tomato paste
- 1 tablespoon granulated stevia
- ¼ teaspoon Worcestershire sauce
- Cooking spray

1. Coat a shallow baking pan with cooking spray.
2. In a large bowl, combine the beaten egg, spinach, onion, milk, salt, almond meal, sage, 1 teaspoon of olive oil, and pepper.
3. Crumble the beef over the spinach mixture. Mix well to combine. Divide the meat mixture in half. Shape each half into a loaf. Place the loaves in the prepared pan.
4. In a small bowl, whisk together the tomato paste, Worcestershire sauce, stevia, and remaining 1 teaspoon of olive oil. Spoon half of the sauce over each meatloaf.
5. Place the pan on the bake position.
6. Select Bake. Set the temperature to 350°F (180°C) and set the time to 40 minutes.
7. When cooking is complete, an instant-read thermometer inserted in the center of the meatloaves should read at least 165°F (74°C).
8. Serve immediately.

Tangy Pork Ribs

Prep time: 1 hour 10 minutes | Cook time: 25 minutes | Serves 6

- 2½ pounds (1.1 kg) boneless country-style pork ribs, cut into 2-inch pieces
- 3 tablespoons olive brine
- 1 tablespoon minced fresh oregano leaves
- ⅓ cup orange juice
- 1 teaspoon ground cumin
- 1 tablespoon minced garlic
- 1 teaspoon salt
- 1 teaspoon ground black pepper
- Cooking spray

1. Combine all the ingredients in a large bowl. Toss to coat the pork ribs well. Wrap the bowl in plastic and refrigerate for at least an hour to marinate.
2. Spritz the air fry basket with cooking spray.
3. Arrange the marinated pork ribs in the basket and spritz with cooking spray.
4. Place the basket on the air fry position.
5. Select Air Fry. Set temperature to 400ºF (205ºC) and set time to 25 minutes. Flip the ribs halfway through.
6. When cooking is complete, the ribs should be well browned.
7. Serve immediately.

Smoked Paprika Pork and Vegetable Kabobs

Prep time: 25 minutes | Cook time: 15 minutes | Serves 4

- 1 pound (454 g) pork tenderloin, cubed
- 1 teaspoon smoked paprika
- Salt and ground black pepper, to taste
- 1 green bell pepper, cut into chunks
- 1 zucchini, cut into chunks
- 1 red onion, sliced
- 1 tablespoon oregano
- Cooking spray

Special Equipment:
- Small bamboo skewers, soaked in water for 20 minutes to keep them from burning while cooking

1. Spritz the air fry basket with cooking spray.
2. Add the pork to a bowl and season with the salt, black pepper, and smoked paprika. Thread the seasoned pork cubes and vegetables alternately onto the soaked skewers. Arrange the skewers in the basket.
3. Place the basket on the air fry position.

4. Select Air Fry. Set temperature to 350ºF (180ºC) and set time to 15 minutes.
5. After 7 minutes, remove the basket from the air fryer grill. Flip the pork skewers. Return the basket to the air fryer grill and continue cooking.
6. When cooking is complete, the pork should be browned and vegetables are tender.
7. Transfer the skewers to the serving dishes and sprinkle with oregano. Serve hot.

Char Siu (Chinese BBQ Pork)

Prep time: 8 hours 10 minutes | Cook time: 15 minutes | Serves 4

- ¼ cup honey
- 1 teaspoon Chinese five-spice powder
- 1 tablespoon Shaoxing wine (rice cooking wine)
- 1 tablespoon hoisin sauce
- 2 teaspoons minced garlic
- 2 teaspoons minced fresh ginger
- 2 tablespoons soy sauce
- 1 tablespoon sugar
- 1 pound (454 g) fatty pork shoulder, cut into long, 1-inch-thick pieces
- Cooking spray

1. Combine all the ingredients, except for the pork should, in a microwave-safe bowl. Stir to mix well. Microwave until the honey has dissolved. Stir periodically.
2. Pierce the pork pieces generously with a fork, then put the pork in a large bowl. Pour in half of the honey mixture. Set the remaining sauce aside until ready to serve.
3. Press the pork pieces into the mixture to coat and wrap the bowl in plastic and refrigerate to marinate for at least 8 hours.
4. Spritz the air fry basket with cooking spray.
5. Discard the marinade and transfer the pork pieces in the air fry basket.
6. Place the basket on the air fry position.
7. Select Air Fry. Set temperature to 400ºF (205ºC) and set time to 15 minutes. Flip the pork halfway through.
8. When cooking is complete, the pork should be well browned.
9. Meanwhile, microwave the remaining marinade on high for a minute or until it has a thick consistency. Stir periodically.
10. Remove the pork from the air fryer grill and allow to cool for 10 minutes before serving with the thickened marinade.

Chapter 5

Poultry

44	Baked Whole Chicken
44	Perpper-Onion Stuffed Chicken Rolls
45	Cheesy Chicken Cubes Pizza
45	Easy China Spicy Turkey Thighs
46	Marmalade Balsamic Glazed Duck Breasts
46	Lime Chicken Breasts with Cilantro
47	Indian Spicy Chicken Drumsticks
47	Japanese Yakitori
48	Peach and Cherry Chicken Chunks
49	Teriyaki Chicken Thighs with Snow Peas
50	Chicken Tenders with Mushroom Sauce
51	Dijon Turkey Cheese Burgers

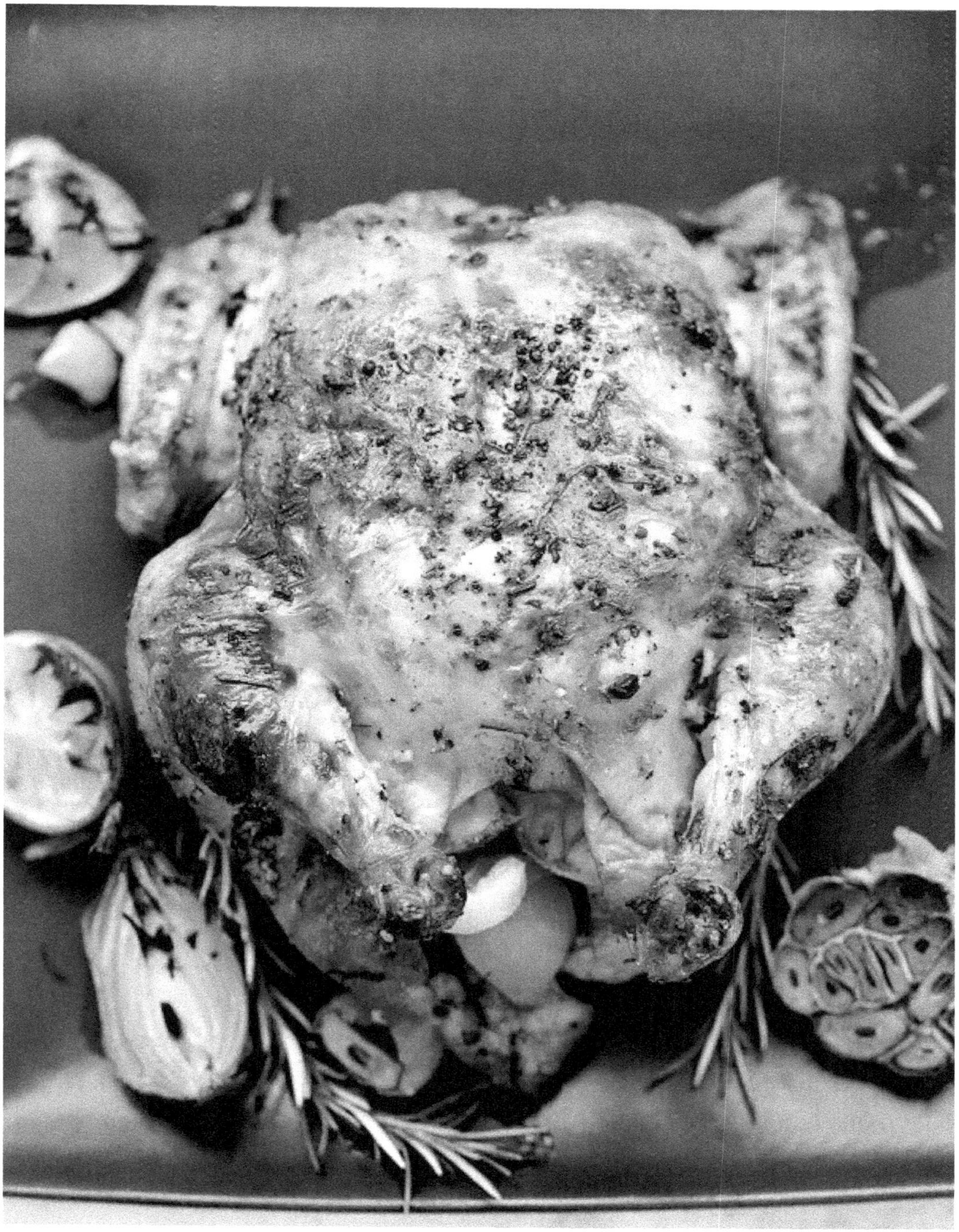

Baked Whole Chicken

Prep time: 10 minutes | Cook time: 1 hour | Serves 2 to 4

- ½ cup melted butter
- 3 tablespoons garlic, minced
- Salt, to taste
- 1 teaspoon ground black pepper
- 1 (1-pound / 454-g) whole chicken

1. Combine the butter with salt, garlic, and ground black pepper in a small bowl.
2. Brush the butter mixture over the whole chicken, then place the chicken in the air fry basket, skin side down.
3. Place the basket on the bake position.
4. Select Bake, set temperature to 350ºF (180ºC) and set time to 60 minutes. Flip the chicken halfway through.
5. When cooking is complete, an instant-read thermometer inserted in the thickest part of the chicken should register at least 165ºF (74ºC).
6. Remove the chicken from the air fryer grill and allow to cool for 15 minutes before serving.

Perpper-Onion Stuffed Chicken Rolls

Prep time: 10 minutes | Cook time: 12 minutes | Serves 4

- 2 (4-ounce / 113-g) boneless, skinless chicken breasts, slice in half horizontally
- 1 tablespoon olive oil
- Juice of ½ lime
- 2 tablespoons taco seasoning
- ½ green bell pepper, cut into strips
- ½ red bell pepper, cut into strips
- ¼ onion, sliced

1. Unfold the chicken breast slices on a clean work surface. Rub with olive oil, then drizzle with lime juice and sprinkle with taco seasoning.
2. Top the chicken slices with equal amount of bell peppers and onion. Roll them up and secure with toothpicks.
3. Arrange the chicken roll-ups in the air fry basket.
4. Place the basket on the air fry position.
5. Select Air Fry. Set temperature to 400ºF (205ºC) and set time to 12 minutes. Flip the chicken roll-ups halfway through.
6. When cooking is complete, the internal temperature of the chicken should reach at least 165ºF (74ºC).
7. Remove the chicken from the air fryer grill. Discard the toothpicks and serve immediately.

Cheesy Chicken Cubes Pizza

Prep time: 15 minutes | Cook time: 15 minutes | Serves 6

- 2 cups cooked chicken, cubed
- 1 cup pizza sauce
- 20 slices pepperoni
- ¼ cup grated Parmesan cheese
- 1 cup shredded Mozzarella cheese
- Cooking spray

1. Spritz a baking pan with cooking spray.
2. Arrange the chicken cubes in the prepared baking pan, then top the cubes with pizza sauce and pepperoni. Stir to coat the cubes and pepperoni with sauce. Scatter the cheeses on top.
3. Place the pan into the air fryer grill.
4. Select Air Fry. Set temperature to 375°F (190°C) and set time to 15 minutes.
5. When cooking is complete, the pizza should be frothy and the cheeses should be melted.
6. Serve immediately.

Easy China Spicy Turkey Thighs

Prep time: 10 minutes | Cook time: 25 minutes | Serves 6

- 2 pounds (907 g) turkey thighs
- 1 teaspoon Chinese five-spice powder
- ¼ teaspoon Sichuan pepper
- 1 teaspoon pink Himalayan salt
- 1 tablespoon Chinese rice vinegar
- 1 tablespoon mustard
- 1 tablespoon chili sauce
- 2 tablespoons soy sauce
- Cooking spray

1. Spritz the air fry basket with cooking spray.
2. Rub the turkey thighs with Sichuan pepper, five-spice powder, and salt on a clean work surface.
3. Put the turkey thighs in the air fry basket and spritz with cooking spray.
4. Place the basket on the air fry position.
5. Select Air Fry. Set temperature to 360°F (182°C) and set time to 22 minutes. Flip the thighs at least three times during the cooking.
6. When cooking is complete, the thighs should be well browned.
7. Meanwhile, heat the remaining ingredients in a saucepan over medium-high heat. Cook for 3 minutes or until the sauce is thickened and reduces to two thirds.
8. Transfer the thighs onto a plate and baste with sauce before serving.

Marmalade Balsamic Glazed Duck Breasts

Prep time: 5 minutes | Cook time: 13 minutes | Serves 4

- 4 (6-ounce / 170-g) skin-on duck breasts
- 1 teaspoon salt
- ¼ cup orange marmalade
- 1 tablespoon white balsamic vinegar
- ¾ teaspoon ground black pepper

1. Cut 10 slits into the skin of the duck breasts, then sprinkle with salt on both sides.
2. Place the breasts in the air fry basket, skin side up.
3. Place the basket on the air fry position.
4. Select Air Fry. Set temperature to 400ºF (205ºC) and set time to 10 minutes.
5. Meanwhile, combine the remaining ingredients in a small bowl. Stir to mix well.
6. When cooking is complete, brush the duck skin with the marmalade mixture. Flip the breast and air fry for 3 more minutes or until the skin is crispy and the breast is well browned.
7. Serve immediately.

Lime Chicken Breasts with Cilantro

Prep time: 35 minutes | Cook time: 10 minutes | Serves 4

- 4 (4-ounce / 113-g) boneless, skinless chicken breasts
- ½ cup chopped fresh cilantro
- Juice of 1 lime
- Chicken seasoning or rub, to taste
- Salt and ground black pepper, to taste
- Cooking spray

1. Put the chicken breasts in the large bowl, then add the cilantro, lime juice, chicken seasoning, salt, and black pepper. Toss to coat well.
2. Wrap the bowl in plastic and refrigerate to marinate for at least 30 minutes.
3. Spritz the air fry basket with cooking spray.
4. Remove the marinated chicken breasts from the bowl and place in the air fry basket. Spritz with cooking spray.
5. Place the basket on the air fry position.
6. Select Air Fry. Set temperature to 400ºF (205ºC) and set time to 10 minutes. Flip the breasts halfway through.
7. When cooking is complete, the internal temperature of the chicken should reach at least 165ºF (74ºC).
8. Serve immediately.

Indian Spicy Chicken Drumsticks

Prep time: 70 minutes | Cook time: 14 minutes | Serves 4

- 8 (4- to 5-ounce / 113- to 142-g) skinless bone-in chicken drumsticks
- ½ cup plain full-fat or low-fat yogurt
- ¼ cup buttermilk
- 2 teaspoons minced garlic
- 2 teaspoons minced fresh ginger
- 2 teaspoons ground cinnamon
- 2 teaspoons ground coriander
- 2 teaspoons mild paprika
- 1 teaspoon salt
- 1 teaspoon Tabasco hot red pepper sauce

1. In a large bowl, stir together all the ingredients except for chicken drumsticks until well combined. Add the chicken drumsticks to the bowl and toss until well coated. Cover in plastic and set in the refrigerator to marinate for 1 hour, tossing once.
2. Arrange the marinated drumsticks in the air fry basket, leaving enough space between them.
3. Place the basket on the air fry position.
4. Select Air Fry. Set temperature to 375ºF (190ºC) and set time to 14 minutes. Flip the drumsticks once halfway through to ensure even cooking.
5. When cooking is complete, the internal temperature of the chicken drumsticks should reach 160ºF (71ºC) on a meat thermometer.
6. Transfer the drumsticks to plates. Rest for 5 minutes before serving.

Japanese Yakitori

Prep time: 10 minutes | Cook time: 15 minutes | Serves 4

- ½ cup mirin
- ¼ cup dry white wine
- ½ cup soy sauce
- 1 tablespoon light brown sugar
- 1½ pounds (680 g) boneless, skinless chicken thighs, cut into 1½-inch pieces, fat trimmed
- 4 medium scallions, trimmed, cut into 1½-inch pieces
- Cooking spray

Special Equipment:
- 4 (4-inch) bamboo skewers, soaked in water for at least 30 minutes

1. Combine the mirin, soy sauce, dry white wine, and brown sugar in a saucepan. Bring to a boil over medium heat. Keep stirring.
2. Boil for another 2 minutes or until it has a thick consistency. Turn off the heat.

3. Spritz the air fry basket with cooking spray.
4. Run the bamboo skewers through the chicken pieces and scallions alternatively.
5. Arrange the skewers in the air fry basket, then brush with mirin mixture on both sides. Spritz with cooking spray.
6. Place the basket on the air fry position.
7. Select Air Fry. Set temperature to 400°F (205°C) and set time to 10 minutes. Flip the skewers halfway through.
8. When cooking is complete, the chicken and scallions should be glossy.
9. Serve immediately.

Peach and Cherry Chicken Chunks

Prep time: 8 minutes | Cook time: 15 minutes | Serves 4

- ⅓ cup peach preserves
- 1 teaspoon ground rosemary
- ½ teaspoon black pepper
- ½ teaspoon salt
- ½ teaspoon marjoram
- 1 teaspoon light olive oil
- 1 pound (454 g) boneless chicken breasts, cut in 1½-inch chunks
- 1 (10-ounce / 284-g) package frozen dark cherries, thawed and drained
- Cooking spray

1. In a medium bowl, mix peach preserves, olive oil, rosemary, marjoram, salt, and pepper.
2. Stir in chicken chunks and toss to coat well with the preserve mixture.
3. Spritz the air fry basket with cooking spray and lay chicken chunks in the air fry basket.
4. Place the basket on the bake position.
5. Select Bake. Set the temperature to 400°F (205°C) and set the time to 15 minutes.
6. After 7 minutes, remove the basket from the air fryer grill. Flip the chicken chunks. Return the basket to the air fryer grill and continue cooking.
7. When cooking is complete, the chicken should no longer pink and the juices should run clear.
8. Scatter the cherries over and cook for an additional minute to heat cherries.
9. Serve immediately.

Teriyaki Chicken Thighs with Snow Peas

Prep time: 30 minutes | Cook time: 34 minutes | Serves 4

- ¼ cup chicken broth
- ½ teaspoon grated fresh ginger
- ⅛ teaspoon red pepper flakes
- 1½ tablespoons soy sauce
- 4 (5-ounce / 142-g) bone-in chicken thighs, trimmed
- 1 tablespoon mirin
- ½ teaspoon cornstarch
- 1 tablespoon sugar
- 6 ounces (170 g) snow peas, strings removed
- ⅛ teaspoon lemon zest
- 1 garlic clove, minced
- ¼ teaspoon salt
- Ground black pepper, to taste
- ½ teaspoon lemon juice

1. Combine the ginger, broth, soy sauce, and pepper flakes in a large bowl. Stir to mix well.
2. Pierce 10 to 15 holes into the chicken skin. Put the chicken in the broth mixture and toss to coat well. Let sit for 10 minutes to marinate.
3. Transfer the marinated chicken on a plate and pat dry with paper towels.
4. Scoop 2 tablespoons of marinade in a microwave-safe bowl and combine with mirin, cornstarch and sugar. Stir to mix well. Microwave for 1 minute or until frothy and has a thick consistency. Set aside.
5. Arrange the chicken in the air fry basket, skin side up.
6. Place the basket on the air fry position. Select Air Fry. Set temperature to 400ºF (205ºC) and set time to 25 minutes. Flip the chicken halfway through.
7. When cooking is complete, brush the chicken skin with marinade mixture. Air fry the chicken for 5 more minutes or until glazed.
8. Remove the chicken from the air fryer grill. Allow the chicken to cool for 10 minutes.
9. Meanwhile, combine the snow peas, lemon zest, garlic, salt, and ground black pepper in a small bowl. Toss to coat well.
10. Transfer the snow peas in the air fry basket.
11. Place the basket on the air fry position. Select Air Fry. Set temperature to 400ºF (205ºC) and set time to 3 minutes.
12. When cooking is complete, the peas should be soft.
13. Remove the peas from the air fryer grill and toss with lemon juice.
14. Serve the chicken with lemony snow peas.

Chicken Tenders with Mushroom Sauce

Prep time: 25 minutes | Cook time: 30 minutes | Serves 4

- 1 tablespoon melted butter
- ¼ cup all-purpose flour
- 4 chicken tenders, cut in half crosswise
- 4 slices ham, ¼-inch thick, large

Mushroom Sauce:
- 2 tablespoons butter
- ½ cup chopped mushrooms
- ½ cup chopped green onions
- 2 tablespoons flour
- enough to cover an English muffin
- 2 English muffins, split in halves
- Salt and ground black pepper, to taste
- Cooking spray
- 1 cup chicken broth
- 1½ teaspoons Worcestershire sauce
- ¼ teaspoon garlic powder

1. Put the butter in a baking pan. Combine the salt, flour, and ground black pepper in a shallow dish. Roll the chicken tenders over to coat well.
2. Arrange the chicken in the baking pan and flip to coat with the melted butter.
3. Place the pan on the broil position.
4. Select Broil, set temperature to 390ºF (199ºC) and set time to 10 minutes. Flip the tenders halfway through.
5. When cooking is complete, the juices of chicken tenders should run clear.
6. Meanwhile, make the mushroom sauce: melt 2 tablespoons of butter in a saucepan over medium-high heat.
7. Add the mushrooms and onions to the saucepan and sauté for 3 minutes or until the onions are translucent.
8. Gently mix in the flour, Worcestershire sauce, garlic powder, and broth until smooth.
9. Reduce the heat to low and simmer for 5 minutes or until it has a thick consistency. Set the sauce aside until ready to serve.
10. When broiling is complete, remove the baking pan from the air fryer grill and set the ham slices into the air fry basket.
11. Select Air Fry. Set time to 5 minutes. Flip the ham slices halfway through.
12. When cooking is complete, the ham slices should be heated through.
13. Remove the ham slices from the air fryer grill and set in the English muffin halves and warm for 1 minute.
14. Arrange each ham slice on top of each muffin half, then place each chicken tender over the ham slice.
15. Transfer to the air fryer grill and set time to 2 minutes on Air Fry.
16. Serve with the sauce on top.

Dijon Turkey Cheese Burgers

Prep time: 10 minutes | Cook time: 25 minutes | Serves 4

- 2 medium yellow onions
- 1 tablespoon olive oil
- 1½ teaspoons kosher salt, divided
- 1¼ pound (567 g) ground turkey
- ⅓ cup mayonnaise
- 1 tablespoon Dijon mustard
- 2 teaspoons Worcestershire sauce
- 4 slices sharp Cheddar cheese (about 4 ounces / 113 g in total)
- 4 hamburger buns, sliced

1. Trim the onions and cut them in half through the root. Cut one of the halves in half. Grate one quarter. Place the grated onion in a large bowl. Thinly slice the remaining onions and place in a medium bowl with the oil and ½ teaspoon of kosher salt. Toss to coat. Place the onions in a single layer on a baking pan.
2. Place the pan on the toast position.
3. Select Toast, set temperature to 350ºF (180ºC), and set time to 10 minutes.
4. While the onions are cooking, add the turkey to the grated onion. Add the remaining kosher salt, Worcestershire sauce, mustard, and mayonnaise. Mix just until combined, being careful not to overwork the turkey. Divide the mixture into 4 patties, each about ¾-inch thick.
5. When cooking is complete, remove the pan from the air fryer grill. Move the onions to one side of the pan and place the burgers on the pan. Poke your finger into the center of each burger to make a deep indentation.
6. Place the pan on the broil position.
7. Select Broil, set temperature to 450ºF (232ºC), and set time to 12 minutes.
8. After 6 minutes, remove the pan. Turn the burgers and stir the onions. Return the pan to the air fryer grill and continue cooking. After about 4 minutes, remove the pan and place the cheese slices on the burgers. Return the pan to the air fryer grill and continue cooking for about 1 minute, or until the cheese is melted and the center of the burgers has reached at least 165ºF (74ºC) on a meat thermometer.
9. When cooking is complete, remove the pan from the air fryer grill. Loosely cover the burgers with foil.
10. Lay out the buns, cut-side up, on the air fryer grill rack. Select Broil, set temperature to 450ºF (232ºC), and set time to 3 minutes. Place the pan on the broil position. Check the buns after 2 minutes; they should be lightly browned.
11. Remove the buns from the air fryer grill. Assemble the burgers and serve.

Chapter 6

Vegan and Vegetarian

- 54 Panko-Crusted Green Beans
- 54 Stuffed Bell Peppers with Cream Cheese
- 55 Easy Ratatouille
- 55 Lemony Brussels Sprouts
- 56 Golden Okra with Chili
- 56 Thai Sweet-Sour Brussels Sprouts
- 57 Toasted Tofu, Carrot and Cauliflower Rice
- 57 Air-Fried Root Vegetable
- 58 Thai Spicy Napa Vegetables
- 59 Crispy Broccoli with Cheese
- 59 Toasted Eggplant, Peppers, Garlic, and Onion
- 60 Honey-Glazed Vegetable

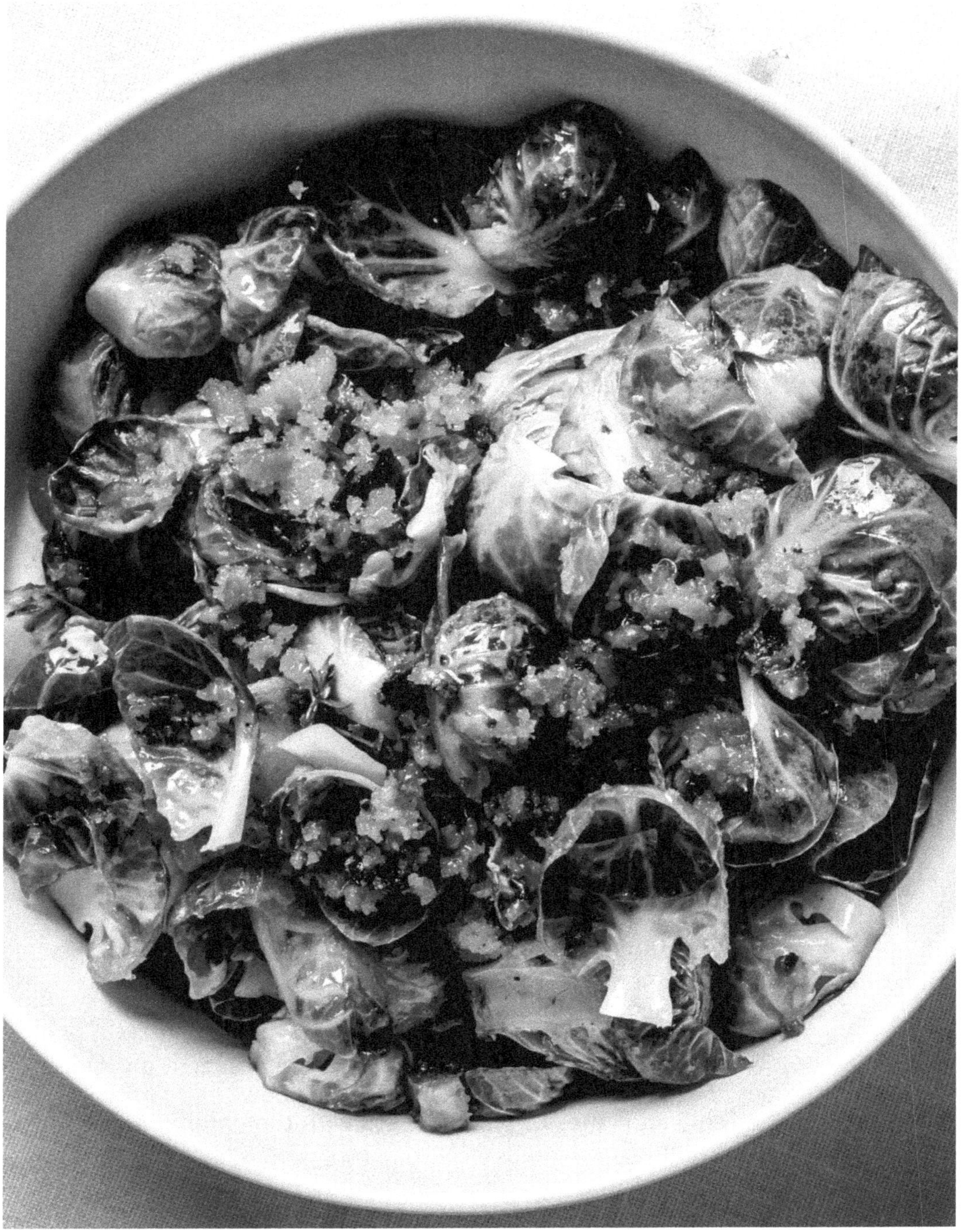

Panko-Crusted Green Beans

Prep time: 5 minutes | Cook time: 15 minutes | Serves 4

- ½ cup flour
- 2 eggs
- 1 cup panko bread crumbs
- ½ cup grated Parmesan cheese
- 1 teaspoon cayenne pepper
- Salt and black pepper, to taste
- 1½ pounds (680 g) green beans

1. In a bowl, place the flour. In a separate bowl, lightly beat the eggs. In a separate shallow bowl, thoroughly combine the bread crumbs, cayenne pepper, cheese, salt, and pepper.
2. Dip the green beans in the flour, then in the beaten eggs, finally in the bread crumb mixture to coat well. Transfer the green beans to the air fry basket.
3. Place the basket on the air fry position.
4. Select Air Fry, set temperature to 400ºF (205ºC), and set time to 15 minutes. Stir the green beans halfway through the cooking time.
5. When cooking is complete, remove from the air fryer grill to a bowl and serve.

Stuffed Bell Peppers with Cream Cheese

Prep time: 5 minutes | Cook time: 15 minutes | Serves 2

- 2 bell peppers, tops and seeds removed
- Salt and pepper, to taste
- ⅔ cup cream cheese
- 2 tablespoons mayonnaise
- 1 tablespoon chopped fresh celery stalks
- Cooking spray

1. Spritz the air fry basket with cooking spray.
2. Place the peppers in the air fry basket.
3. Place the basket on the toast position.
4. Select Toast, set temperature to 400ºF (205ºC) and set time to 10 minutes. Flip the peppers halfway through.
5. When cooking is complete, the peppers should be crisp-tender.
6. Remove from the air fryer grill to a plate and season with salt and pepper.
7. Mix the cream cheese, celery, and mayo in a small bowl and stir to incorporate. Evenly stuff the Toasted peppers with the cream cheese mixture with a spoon. Serve immediately.

Easy Ratatouille

Prep time: 15 minutes | Cook time: 16 minutes | Serves 2

- 2 Roma tomatoes, thinly sliced
- 1 zucchini, thinly sliced
- 2 yellow bell peppers, sliced
- 2 garlic cloves, minced
- 2 tablespoons olive oil
- 2 tablespoons herbes de Prair fryer grillce
- 1 tablespoon vinegar
- Salt and black pepper, to taste

1. Place the tomatoes, bell peppers, garlic, zucchini, olive oil, vinegar, and herbes de Prair fryer grillce in a large bowl and toss until the vegetables are evenly coated. Sprinkle with salt and pepper and toss again. Pour the vegetable mixture into a baking dish.
2. Place the baking dish on the toast position.
3. Select Toast, set temperature to 390°F (199°C) and set time to 16 minutes. Stir the vegetables halfway through.
4. When cooking is complete, the vegetables should be tender.
5. Let the vegetable mixture stand for 5 minutes in the air fryer grill before removing and serving.

Lemony Brussels Sprouts

Prep time: 15 minutes | Cook time: 20 minutes | Serves 4

- 1 pound (454 g) Brussels sprouts, trimmed and halved
- 1 tablespoon extra-virgin olive oil
- Sea Salt and freshly ground black pepper, to taste
- ½ cup sun-dried tomatoes, chopped
- 2 tablespoons freshly squeezed lemon juice
- 1 teaspoon lemon zest

1. Line a large baking sheet with aluminum foil.
2. Toss the Brussels sprouts with the olive oil in a large bowl. Sprinkle with salt and black pepper.
3. Spread the Brussels sprouts in a single layer on the baking sheet.
4. Place the baking sheet on the toast position.
5. Select Toast, set temperature to 400°F (205°C), and set time to 20 minutes.
6. When done, the Brussels sprouts should be caramelized. Remove from the air fryer grill to a serving bowl, along with the tomatoes, lemon juice, and lemon zest. Toss to combine. Serve immediately.

Golden Okra with Chili

Prep time: 5 minutes | Cook time: 10 minutes | Serves 4

- 3 tablespoons sour cream
- 2 tablespoons flour
- 2 tablespoons semolina
- ½ teaspoon red chili powder
- Salt and black pepper, to taste
- 1 pound (454 g) okra, halved
- Cooking spray

1. Spray the air fry basket with cooking spray. Set aside.
2. In a shallow bowl, place the sour cream. In another shallow bowl, thoroughly combine the flour, semolina, red chili powder, salt, and pepper.
3. Dredge the okra in the sour cream, then roll in the flour mixture until evenly coated. Transfer the okra to the air fry basket.
4. Place the basket on the air fry position.
5. Select Air Fry, set temperature to 400ºF (205ºC), and set time to 10 minutes. Flip the okra halfway through the cooking time.
6. When cooking is complete, the okra should be golden brown and crispy. Remove the basket from the air fryer grill. Cool for 5 minutes before serving.

Thai Sweet-Sour Brussels Sprouts

Prep time: 5 minutes | Cook time: 20 minutes | Serves 2

- ¼ cup Thai sweet chili sauce
- 2 tablespoons black vinegar or balsamic vinegar
- ½ teaspoon hot sauce
- 2 small shallots, cut into ¼-inch-thick slices
- 8 ounces (227 g) Brussels sprouts, trimmed (large sprouts halved)
- Kosher salt and freshly ground black pepper, to taste
- 2 teaspoons lightly packed fresh cilantro leaves, for garnish

1. Place the chili sauce, hot sauce, and vinegar in a large bowl and whisk to combine.
2. Add the shallots and Brussels sprouts and toss to coat. Sprinkle with the salt and pepper. Transfer the Brussels sprouts and sauce to a baking pan.
3. Place the pan on the toast position.
4. Select Toast, set temperature to 390ºF (199ºC), and set time to 20 minutes. Stir the Brussels sprouts twice during cooking.
5. When cooking is complete, the Brussels sprouts should be crisp-tender. Remove from the air fryer grill. Sprinkle the cilantro on top for garnish and serve warm.

Toasted Tofu, Carrot and Cauliflower Rice

Prep time: 10 minutes | Cook time: 22 minutes | Serves 4

- ½ block tofu, crumbled
- 1 cup diced carrot
- ½ cup diced onions

Cauliflower:
- 3 cups cauliflower rice
- ½ cup chopped broccoli
- ½ cup frozen peas
- 2 tablespoons soy sauce
- 2 tablespoons soy sauce
- 1 teaspoon turmeric
- 1 tablespoon minced ginger
- 2 garlic cloves, minced
- 1 tablespoon rice vinegar
- 1½ teaspoons toasted sesame oil

1. Mix the carrot, tofu, onions, turmeric, and soy sauce in a baking dish and stir until well incorporated.
2. Place the baking dish on the toast position.
3. Select Toast, set temperature to 370ºF (188ºC) and set time to 10 minutes. Flip the tofu and carrot halfway through the cooking time.
4. When cooking is complete, the tofu should be crisp.
5. Meanwhile, in a large bowl, combine all the ingredients for the cauliflower and toss well.
6. Remove the dish from the air fryer grill and add the cauliflower mixture to the tofu and stir to combine.
7. Return the baking dish to the air fryer grill and set time to 12 minutes on Roast. Place the baking dish on the toast position
8. When cooking is complete, the vegetables should be tender.
9. Cool for 5 minutes before serving.

Air-Fried Root Vegetable

Prep time: 10 minutes | Cook time: 22 minutes | Serves 4

- 2 carrots, sliced
- 2 potatoes, cut into chunks
- 1 rutabaga, cut into chunks
- 1 turnip, cut into chunks
- 1 beet, cut into chunks
- 8 shallots, halved
- 2 tablespoons olive oil
- Salt and black pepper, to taste
- 2 tablespoons tomato pesto
- 2 tablespoons water
- 2 tablespoons chopped fresh thyme

1. Toss the carrots, potatoes, beet, shallots, turnip, rutabaga, olive oil, salt, and pepper in a large mixing bowl until the root vegetables are evenly coated.

2. Place the root vegetables in the air fry basket.
3. Place the basket on the air fry position.
4. Select Air Fry, set temperature to 400ºF (205ºC) and set time to 22 minutes. Stir the vegetables twice during cooking.
5. When cooking is complete, the vegetables should be tender.
6. Meanwhile, in a small bowl, whisk together the tomato pesto and water until smooth.
7. When ready, remove the root vegetables from the air fryer grill to a platter. Drizzle with the tomato pesto mixture and sprinkle with the thyme. Serve immediately.

Thai Spicy Napa Vegetables

Prep time: 10 minutes | Cook time: 8 minutes | Serves 4

- 1 small head Napa cabbage, shredded, divided
- 1 medium carrot, cut into thin coins
- 8 ounces (227 g) snow peas
- 1 red or green bell pepper, sliced into thin strips
- 1 tablespoon vegetable oil
- 2 tablespoons soy sauce
- 1 tablespoon sesame oil
- 2 tablespoons brown sugar
- 2 tablespoons freshly squeezed lime juice
- 2 teaspoons red or green Thai curry paste
- 1 serrano chile, deseeded and minced
- 1 cup frozen mango slices, thawed
- ½ cup chopped Toasted peanuts or cashews

1. Put half the Napa cabbage in a large bowl, along with the carrot, bell pepper, and snow peas. Drizzle with the vegetable oil and toss to coat. Spread them evenly on the sheet pan.
2. Place the pan on the toast position.
3. Select Toast, set temperature to 375ºF (190ºC), and set time to 8 minutes.
4. Meanwhile, whisk together the soy sauce, brown sugar, sesame oil, curry paste, and lime juice in a small bowl.
5. When done, the vegetables should be tender and crisp. Remove the pan and put the vegetables back into the bowl. Add the remaining cabbage, mango slices, and the chile. Pour over the dressing and toss to coat. Top with the Toasted nuts and serve.

Crispy Broccoli with Cheese

Prep time: 5 minutes | Cook time: 18 minutes | Serves 4

- 1 large-sized head broccoli, stemmed and cut into small florets
- 2½ tablespoons canola oil
- 2 teaspoons dried basil
- 2 teaspoons dried rosemary
- Salt and ground black pepper, to taste
- ⅓ cup grated yellow cheese

1. Bring a pot of lightly salted water to a boil. Add the broccoli florets to the boiling water and let boil for about 3 minutes.
2. Drain the broccoli florets well and transfer to a large bowl. Add the canola oil, salt, black pepper, rosemary, and basil to the bowl and toss until the broccoli is fully coated. Place the broccoli in the air fry basket.
3. Place the air fry basket on the air fry position.
4. Select Air Fry, set temperature to 390°F (199°C), and set time to 15 minutes. Stir the broccoli halfway through the cooking time.
5. When cooking is complete, the broccoli should be crisp. Remove the basket from the air fryer grill. Serve the broccoli warm with grated cheese sprinkled on top.

Toasted Eggplant, Peppers, Garlic, and Onion

Prep time: 15 minutes | Cook time: 20 minutes | Serves 2

- 1 small eggplant, halved and sliced
- 1 yellow bell pepper, cut into thick strips
- 1 red bell pepper, cut into thick strips
- 2 garlic cloves, quartered
- 1 red onion, sliced
- 1 tablespoon extra-virgin olive oil
- Salt and freshly ground black pepper, to taste
- ½ cup chopped fresh basil, for garnish
- Cooking spray

1. Grease a nonstick baking dish with cooking spray.
2. Place the eggplant, garlic, red onion, and bell peppers in the greased baking dish. Drizzle with the olive oil and toss to coat well. Spritz any uncoated surfaces with cooking spray.
3. Place the baking dish on the bake position.
4. Select Bake, set temperature to 350°F (180°C), and set time to 20 minutes. Flip the vegetables halfway through the cooking time.
5. When done, remove from the air fryer grill and sprinkle with salt and pepper.
6. Sprinkle the basil on top for garnish and serve.

Honey-Glazed Vegetable

Prep time: 15 minutes | Cook time: 20 minutes | Makes 3 cups

Glaze:
- 2 tablespoons raw honey
- 2 teaspoons minced garlic
- ¼ teaspoon dried marjoram
- ¼ teaspoon dried basil
- ¼ teaspoon dried oregano
- ⅛ teaspoon dried sage
- ⅛ teaspoon dried rosemary
- ⅛ teaspoon dried thyme
- ½ teaspoon salt
- ¼ teaspoon ground black pepper

Veggies:
- 3 to 4 medium red potatoes, cut into 1- to 2-inch pieces
- 1 small zucchini, cut into 1- to 2-inch pieces
- 1 small carrot, sliced into ¼-inch rounds
- 1 (10.5-ounce / 298-g) package cherry tomatoes, halved
- 1 cup sliced mushrooms
- 3 tablespoons olive oil

1. Combine the honey, garlic, basil, marjoram, rosemary, oregano, thyme, sage, salt, and pepper in a small bowl and stir to mix well. Set aside.
2. Place the red potatoes, carrot, cherry tomatoes, zucchini, and mushroom in a large bowl. Drizzle with the olive oil and toss to coat.
3. Pour the veggies into the air fry basket.
4. Place the basket on the toast position.
5. Select Toast, set temperature to 380°F (193°C) and set time to 15 minutes. Stir the veggies halfway through.
6. When cooking is complete, the vegetables should be tender.
7. When ready, transfer the Toasted veggies to the large bowl. Pour the honey mixture over the veggies, tossing to coat.
8. Spread out the veggies in a baking pan and place in the air fryer grill.
9. Increase the temperature to 390°F (199°C) and set time to 5 minutes on Roast. Place the basket on the toast position.
10. When cooking is complete, the veggies should be tender and glazed. Serve warm.

Chapter 7

Vegetable Sides

- **63** Tangy Sweet Potatoes
- **63** Golden Cheesy Corn Casserole
- **64** Russet Potatoes with Yogurt and Chives
- **64** Crispy Zucchini Rounds
- **65** Blistered Shishito Peppers with Lime Sauce

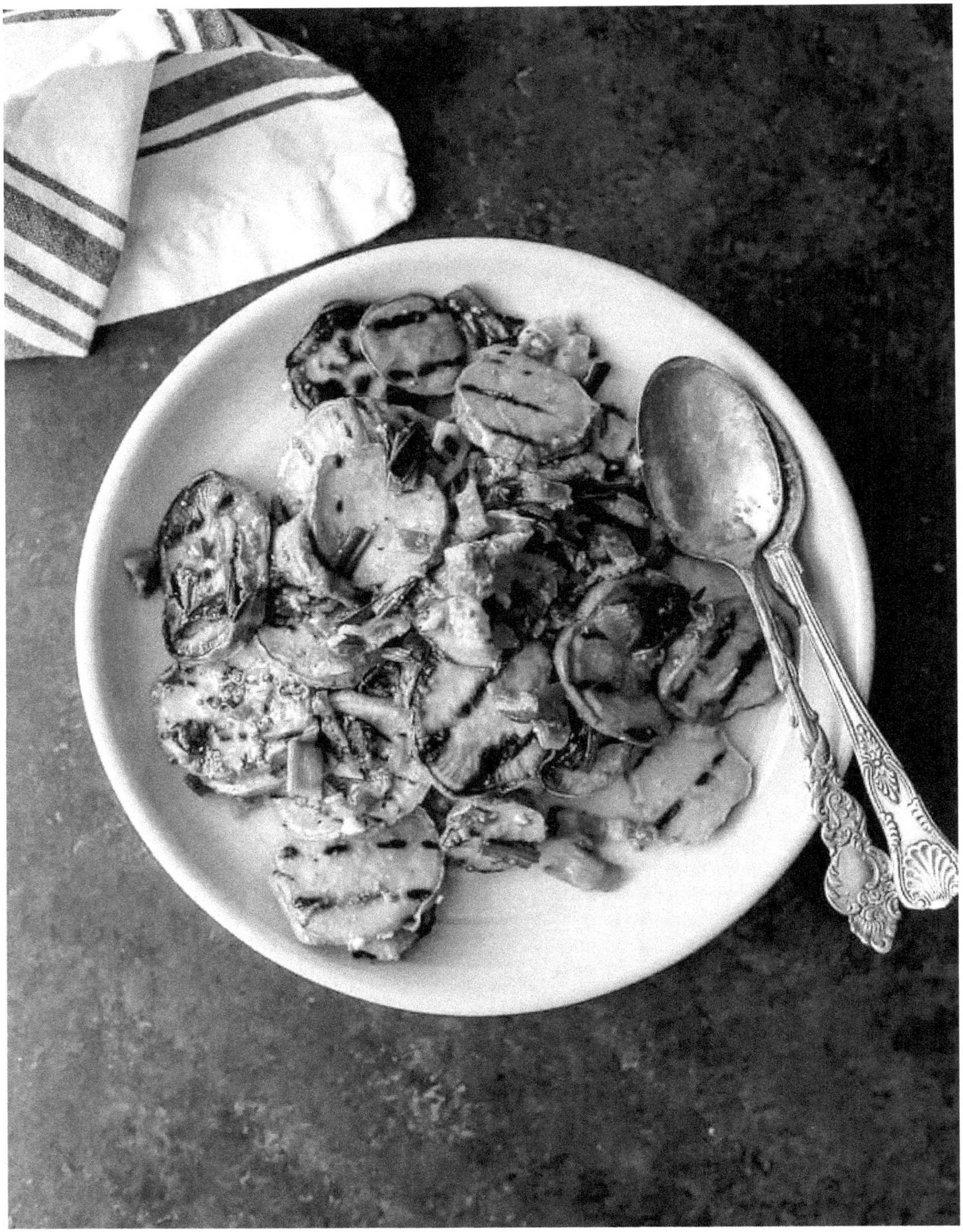

Tangy Sweet Potatoes

Prep time: 5 minutes | Cook time: 22 minutes | Serves 4

- 5 garnet sweet potatoes, peeled and diced
- 1½ tablespoons fresh lime juice
- 1 tablespoon butter, melted
- 2 teaspoons tamarind paste
- 1½ teaspoon ground allspice
- ⅓ teaspoon white pepper
- ½ teaspoon turmeric powder
- A few drops liquid stevia

1. In a large mixing bowl, combine all the ingredients and toss until the sweet potatoes are evenly coated. Place the sweet potatoes in the air fry basket.
2. Place the basket on the air fry position.
3. Select Air Fry, set temperature to 400ºF (205ºC), and set time to 22 minutes. Stir the potatoes twice during cooking.
4. When cooking is complete, the potatoes should be crispy on the outside and soft on the inside. Let the potatoes cool for 5 minutes before serving.

Golden Cheesy Corn Casserole

Prep time: 5 minutes | Cook time: 15 minutes | Serves 4

- 2 cups frozen yellow corn
- 1 egg, beaten
- 3 tablespoons flour
- ½ cup grated Swiss or Havarti cheese
- ½ cup light cream
- ¼ cup milk
- Pinch salt
- Freshly ground black pepper, to taste
- 2 tablespoons butter, cut into cubes
- Nonstick cooking spray

1. Spritz a baking pan with nonstick cooking spray.
2. Stir together the remaining ingredients except the butter in a medium bowl until well incorporated. Transfer the mixture to the prepared baking pan and scatter with the butter cubes.
3. Place the pan on the bake position.
4. Select Bake, set temperature to 320ºF (160ºC), and set time to 15 minutes.
5. When cooking is complete, the top should be golden brown and a toothpick inserted in the center should come out clean. Remove the pan from the air fryer grill. Let the casserole cool for 5 minutes before slicing into wedges and serving.

Russet Potatoes with Yogurt and Chives

Prep time: 5 minutes | Cook time: 35 minutes | Serves 4

- 4 (7-ounce / 198-g) russet potatoes, rinsed
- Olive oil spray
- ½ teaspoon kosher salt, divided
- ½ cup 2% plain Greek yogurt
- ¼ cup minced fresh chives
- Freshly ground black pepper, to taste

1. Pat the potatoes dry and pierce them all over with a fork. Spritz the potatoes with olive oil spray. Sprinkle with ¼ teaspoon of the salt.
2. Transfer the potatoes to the air fry basket.
3. Place the basket on the bake position.
4. Select Bake, set temperature to 400°F (205°C), and set time to 35 minutes.
5. When cooking is complete, the potatoes should be fork-tender. Remove from the air fryer grill and split open the potatoes. Top with the chives, yogurt, the remaining ¼ teaspoon of salt, and finish with the black pepper. Serve immediately.

Crispy Zucchini Rounds

Prep time: 5 minutes | Cook time: 14 minutes | Serves 4

- 2 zucchini, sliced into ¼- to ½-inch-thick rounds (about 2 cups)
- ¼ teaspoon garlic granules
- ⅛ teaspoon sea salt
- Freshly ground black pepper, to taste (optional)
- Cooking spray

1. Spritz the air fry basket with cooking spray.
2. Put the zucchini rounds in the air fry basket, spreading them out as much as possible. Top with a sprinkle of sea salt, garlic granules, and black pepper (if desired). Spritz the zucchini rounds with cooking spray.
3. Place the basket on the toast position.
4. Select Toast, set temperature to 392°F (200°C), and set time to 14 minutes. Flip the zucchini rounds halfway through.
5. When cooking is complete, the zucchini rounds should be crisp-tender. Remove from the air fryer grill. Let them rest for 5 minutes and serve.

Blistered Shishito Peppers with Lime Sauce

Prep time: 5 minutes | Cook time: 9 minutes | Serves 3

- ½ pound (227 g) shishito peppers, rinsed
- Cooking spray

Sauce:
- 1 tablespoon tamari or shoyu
- 2 teaspoons fresh lime juice
- 2 large garlic cloves, minced

1. Spritz the air fry basket with cooking spray.
2. Place the shishito peppers in the air fry basket and spritz them with cooking spray.
3. Place the basket on the toast position.
4. Select Toast, set temperature to 392ºF (200ºC), and set time to 9 minutes.
5. Meanwhile, whisk together all the ingredients for the sauce in a large bowl. Set aside.
6. After 3 minutes, remove the basket from the air fryer grill. Flip the peppers and spritz them with cooking spray. Return to the air fryer grill and continue cooking.
7. After another 3 minutes, remove the basket from the air fryer grill. Flip the peppers and spray with cooking spray. Return to the air fryer grill and continue roasting for 3 minutes more, or until the peppers are blistered and nicely browned.
8. When cooking is complete, remove the peppers from the air fryer grill to the bowl of sauce. Toss to coat well and serve immediately.

Chapter 8

Appetizers and Snacks

- 68   Spicy Potato Chips
- 68   Crunchy Cinnamon Apple Chips
- 69   Sweet-Salty Mixed Snack
- 69   Cheesy Sausage Balls
- 70   Garlicky Toasted Mushrooms

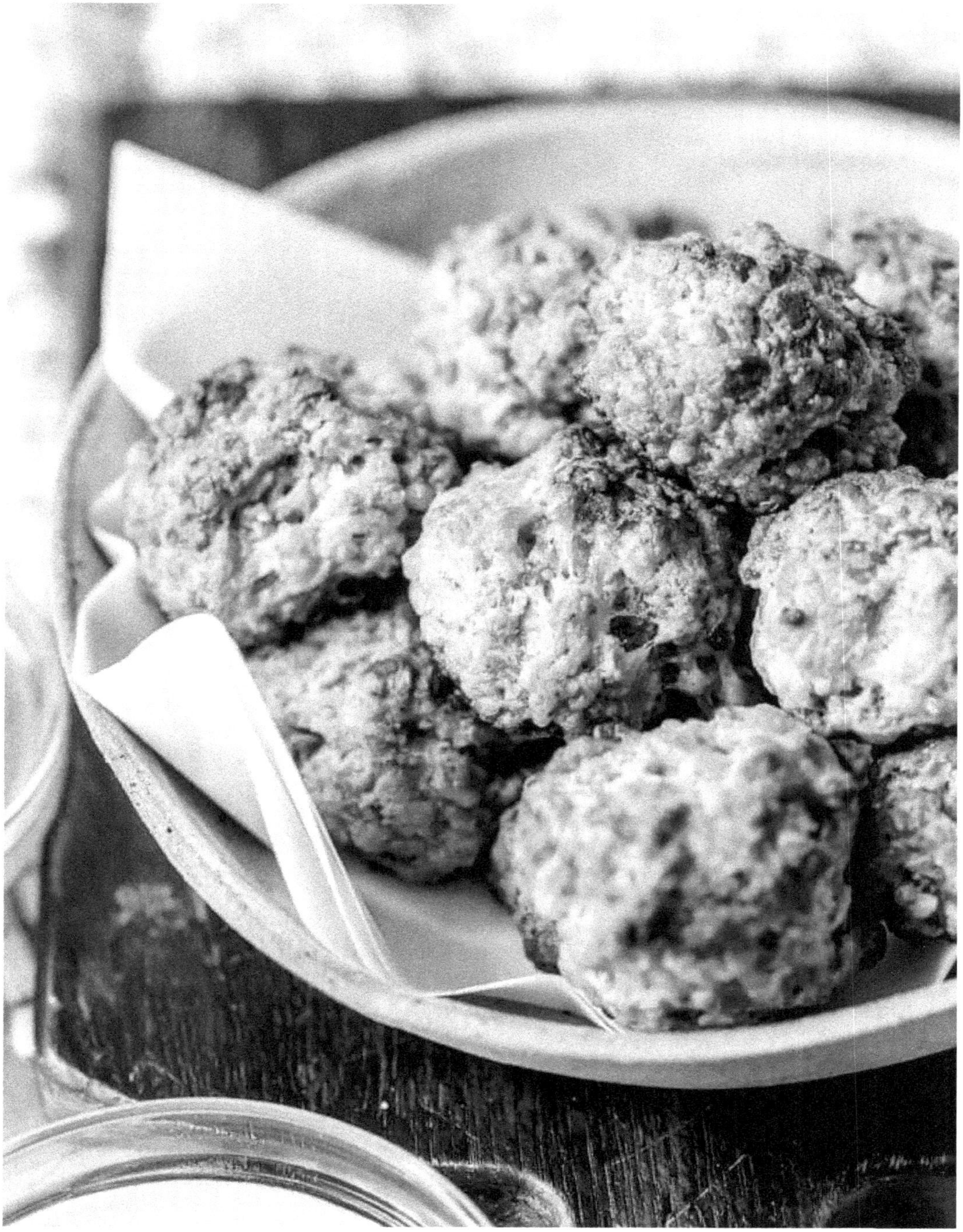

Spicy Potato Chips

Prep time: 5 minutes | Cook time: 22 minutes | Serves 3

- 2 medium potatoes, preferably Yukon Gold, scrubbed
- Cooking spray
- 2 teaspoons olive oil
- ½ teaspoon garlic granules
- ¼ teaspoon paprika
- ¼ teaspoon plus ⅛ teaspoon sea salt
- ¼ teaspoon freshly ground black pepper
- Ketchup or hot sauce, for serving

1. Spritz the air fry basket with cooking spray.
2. On a flat work surface, cut the potatoes into ¼-inch-thick slices. Transfer the potato slices to a medium bowl, along with the garlic granules, paprika, olive oil, salt, and pepper and toss to coat well. Transfer the potato slices to the air fry basket.
3. Place the basket on the air fry position.
4. Select Air Fry, set temperature to 392ºF (200ºC), and set time to 22 minutes. Stir the potato slices twice during the cooking process.
5. When cooking is complete, the potato chips should be tender and nicely browned. Remove from the air fryer grill and serve alongside the ketchup for dipping.

Crunchy Cinnamon Apple Chips

Prep time: 10 minutes | Cook time: 10 minutes | Serves 4

- 2 apples, cored and cut into thin slices
- 2 heaped teaspoons ground cinnamon
- Cooking spray

1. Spritz the air fry basket with cooking spray.
2. In a medium bowl, sprinkle the apple slices with the cinnamon. Toss until evenly coated. Spread the coated apple slices on the pan in a single layer.
3. Place the basket on the air fry position.
4. Select Air Fry, set temperature to 350ºF (180ºC) and set time to 10 minutes.
5. After 5 minutes, remove the basket from the air fryer grill. Stir the apple slices and return the basket to the air fryer grill to continue cooking.
6. When cooking is complete, the slices should be until crispy Remove the basket from the air fryer grill and let rest for 5 minutes before serving.

Sweet-Salty Mixed Snack

Prep time: 5 minutes | Cook time: 10 minutes | Makes about 10 cups

- 3 tablespoons butter, melted
- ½ cup honey
- 1 teaspoon salt
- 2 cups granola
- 2 cups sesame sticks
- 2 cups crispy corn puff cereal
- 2 cups mini pretzel crisps
- 1 cup cashews
- 1 cup pepitas
- 1 cup dried cherries

1. In a small mixing bowl, mix together the butter, honey, and salt until well incorporated.
2. In a large bowl, combine the sesame sticks, granola, cashews, corn puff cereal and pretzel crisps, and pepitas. Drizzle with the butter mixture and toss until evenly coated. Transfer the snack mix to a sheet pan.
3. Slide the pan into the air fryer grill.
4. Select Air Fry, set temperature to 370ºF (188ºC), and set time to 10 minutes. Stir the snack mix halfway through the cooking time.
5. When cooking is complete, they should be lightly toasted. Remove from the air fryer grill and allow to cool completely. Scatter with the dried cherries and mix well. Serve immediately.

Cheesy Sausage Balls

Prep time: 10 minutes | Cook time: 10 minutes | Serves 8

- 12 ounces (340 g) mild ground sausage
- 1½ cups baking mix
- 1 cup shredded mild Cheddar cheese
- 3 ounces (85 g) cream cheese, at room temperature
- 1 to 2 tablespoons olive oil

1. Line the air fry basket with parchment paper. Set aside.
2. Mix together the ground sausage, Cheddar cheese, cream cheese, and baking mix in a large bowl and stir to incorporate.
3. Divide the sausage mixture into 16 equal portions and roll them into 1-inch balls with your hands. Arrange the sausage balls on the parchment, leaving space between each ball. Brush the sausage balls with the olive oil.
4. Place the basket on the air fry position.
5. Select Air Fry, set temperature to 325ºF (163ºC), and set time to 10 minutes. Flip the balls halfway through the cooking time.
6. When cooking is complete, the balls should be firm and lightly browned on both sides. Remove from the air fryer grill to a plate and serve warm.

Garlicky Toasted Mushrooms

Prep time: 5 minutes | Cook time: 27 minutes | Serves 4

- 16 garlic cloves, peeled
- 2 teaspoons olive oil, divided
- 16 button mushrooms
- ½ teaspoon dried marjoram
- ⅛ teaspoon freshly ground black pepper
- 1 tablespoon white wine

1. Place the garlic cloves on the sheet pan and drizzle with 1 teaspoon of the olive oil. Toss to coat well.
2. Place the pan on the toast position.
3. Select Toast, set temperature to 350ºF (180ºC) and set time to 12 minutes.
4. When cooking is complete, remove the pan from the air fryer grill. Stir in the mushrooms, pepper and marjoram. Drizzle with the remaining 1 teaspoon of the olive oil and the white wine. Toss to coat well. Return the pan to the air fryer grill.
5. Place the pan on the toast position.
6. Select Toast, set temperature to 350ºF (180ºC) and set time to 15 minutes.
7. Once done, the mushrooms and garlic cloves will be softened. Remove the pan from the air fryer grill.
8. Serve warm.

Chapter 9

Desserts

- 73   Sweet Strawberry and Rhubarb Crumble
- 73   Vanilla Chocolate Cookies
- 74   Berries with Nuts Streusel Topping
- 75   Middle East Baklava
- 76   Coffee Cake

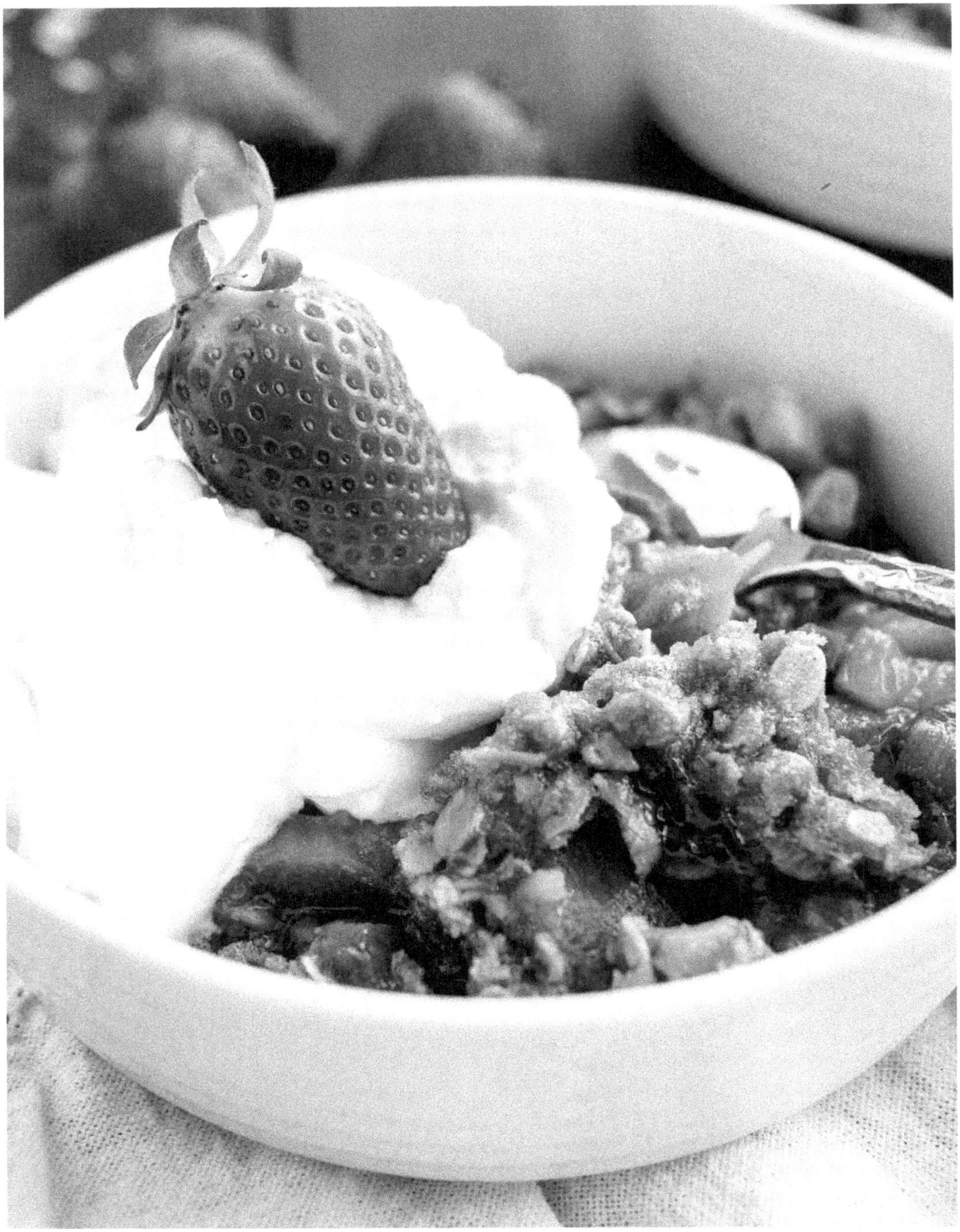

Sweet Strawberry and Rhubarb Crumble

Prep time: 10 minutes | Cook time: 12 to 17 minutes | Serves 6

- 1½ cups sliced fresh strawberries
- ⅓ cup sugar
- ¾ cup sliced rhubarb
- ⅔ cup quick-cooking oatmeal
- ¼ cup packed brown sugar
- ½ cup whole-wheat pastry flour
- ½ teaspoon ground cinnamon
- 3 tablespoons unsalted butter, melted

1. Place the rhubarb, strawberries, and sugar in a baking pan and toss to coat.
2. Combine the oatmeal, pastry flour, cinnamon, and brown sugar in a medium bowl.
3. Add the melted butter to the oatmeal mixture and stir until crumbly. Sprinkle this generously on top of the strawberries and rhubarb.
4. Place the pan on the bake position.
5. Select Bake, set temperature to 370ºF (188ºC), and set the time to 12 minutes.
6. Bake until the fruit is bubbly and the topping is golden brown. Continue cooking for an additional 2 to 5 minutes if needed.
7. When cooking is complete, remove from the air fryer grill and serve warm.

Vanilla Chocolate Cookies

Prep time: 10 minutes | Cook time: 22 minutes | Makes 30 cookies

- ⅓ cup (80g) organic brown sugar
- ⅓ cup (80g) organic cane sugar
- 4 ounces (112g) cashew-based vegan butter
- ½ cup coconut cream
- 1 teaspoon vanilla extract
- 2 tablespoons ground flaxseed
- 1 teaspoon baking powder
- 1 teaspoon baking soda
- Pinch of salt
- 2¼ cups (220g) almond flour
- ½ cup (90g) dairy-free dark chocolate chips

1. Line a baking sheet with parchment paper.
2. Mix together the brown sugar, cane sugar, and butter in a medium bowl or the bowl of a stand mixer. Cream together with a mixer.
3. Fold in the vanilla, coconut cream, flaxseed, baking soda, baking powder, and salt. Stir well.

4. Add the almond flour, a little at a time, mixing after each addition until fully incorporated. Stir in the chocolate chips with a spatula.
5. Scoop the dough onto the prepared baking sheet.
6. Place the baking sheet on the bake position.
7. Select Bake, set temperature to 325°F (160°C), and set the time to 22 minutes.
8. Bake until the cookies are golden brown.
9. When cooking is complete, transfer the baking sheet onto a wire rack to cool completely before serving.

Berries with Nuts Streusel Topping

Prep time: 5 minutes | Cook time: 17 minutes | Serves 3

- ½ cup mixed berries

Topping:
- 1 egg, beaten
- 3 tablespoons almonds, slivered
- 3 tablespoons chopped pecans
- 2 tablespoons chopped walnuts
- Cooking spray
- 3 tablespoons granulated Swerve
- 2 tablespoons cold salted butter, cut into pieces
- ½ teaspoon ground cinnamon

1. Lightly spray a baking dish with cooking spray.
2. Make the topping: In a medium bowl, stir together the beaten egg, nuts, butter, cinnamon, and Swerve until well blended.
3. Put the mixed berries in the bottom of the baking dish and spread the topping over the top.
4. Place the baking dish on the bake position.
5. Select Bake, set temperature to 340ºF (171ºC), and set time to 17 minutes.
6. When cooking is complete, the fruit should be bubbly and topping should be golden brown.
7. Allow to cool for 5 to 10 minutes before serving.

Middle East Baklava

Prep time: 10 minutes | Cook time: 16 minutes | Serves 10

- 1 cup walnut pieces
- 1 cup shelled raw pistachios
- ½ cup unsalted butter, melted
- ¼ cup plus 2 tablespoons honey, divided
- 3 tablespoons granulated sugar
- 1 teaspoon ground cinnamon
- 2 (1.9-ounce / 54-g) packages frozen miniature phyllo tart shells

1. Place the walnuts and pistachios in the air fry basket in an even layer.
2. Place the basket on the air fry position.
3. Select Air Fry, set the temperature to 350ºF (180ºC), and set the time for 4 minutes.
4. After 2 minutes, remove the basket and stir the nuts. Transfer the basket back to the air fryer grill and cook for another 1 to 2 minutes until the nuts are golden brown and fragrant.
5. Meanwhile, stir together the butter, sugar, cinnamon, and ¼ cup of honey in a medium bowl.
6. When done, remove the basket from the air fryer grill and place the nuts on a cutting board and allow to cool for 5 minutes. Finely chop the nuts. Add the chopped nuts and all the "nut dust" to the butter mixture and stir well.
7. Arrange the phyllo cups on the basket. Evenly fill the phyllo cups with the nut mixture, mounding it up. As you work, stir the nuts in the bowl frequently so that the syrup is evenly distributed throughout the filling.
8. Place the basket on the bake position.
9. Select Bake, set temperature to 350ºF (180ºC), and set time to 12 minutes. After about 8 minutes, check the cups. Continue cooking until the cups are golden brown and the syrup is bubbling.
10. When cooking is complete, remove the baklava from the air fryer grill, drizzle each cup with about ⅛ teaspoon of the remaining honey over the top.
11. Allow to cool for 5 minutes before serving.

Coffee Cake

Prep time: 5 minutes | Cook time: 30 minutes | Serves 8

Dry Ingredients:
- 1½ cups almond flour
- ½ cup coconut meal
- ⅔ cup Swerve
- 1 teaspoon baking powder
- ¼ teaspoon salt

Wet Ingredients:
- 1 egg
- 1 stick butter, melted
- ½ cup hot strongly brewed coffee

Topping:
- ½ cup confectioner's Swerve
- ¼ cup coconut flour
- 3 tablespoons coconut oil
- 1 teaspoon ground cinnamon
- ½ teaspoon ground cardamom

1. In a medium bowl, combine the almond flour, salt, baking powder, coconut meal, and Swerve.
2. In a large bowl, whisk the melted butter, egg, and coffee until smooth.
3. Add the dry mixture to the wet and stir until well incorporated. Transfer the batter to a greased baking pan.
4. Stir together all the ingredients for the topping in a small bowl. Spread the topping over the batter and smooth the top with a spatula.
5. Place the pan on the bake position.
6. Select Bake, set temperature to 330ºF (166ºC), and set time to 30 minutes.
7. When cooking is complete, the cake should spring back when gently pressed with your fingers.
8. Rest for 10 minutes before serving.

Chapter 10

Casseroles, Frittata, and Quiche

79	Lush Vegetable Frittata
79	Burgundy Steak and Mushroom Casserole
80	Fast Chicken Sausage and Broccoli Casserole
81	Cheesy Keto Quiche
82	Hearty Pimento and Almond Turkey Casserole

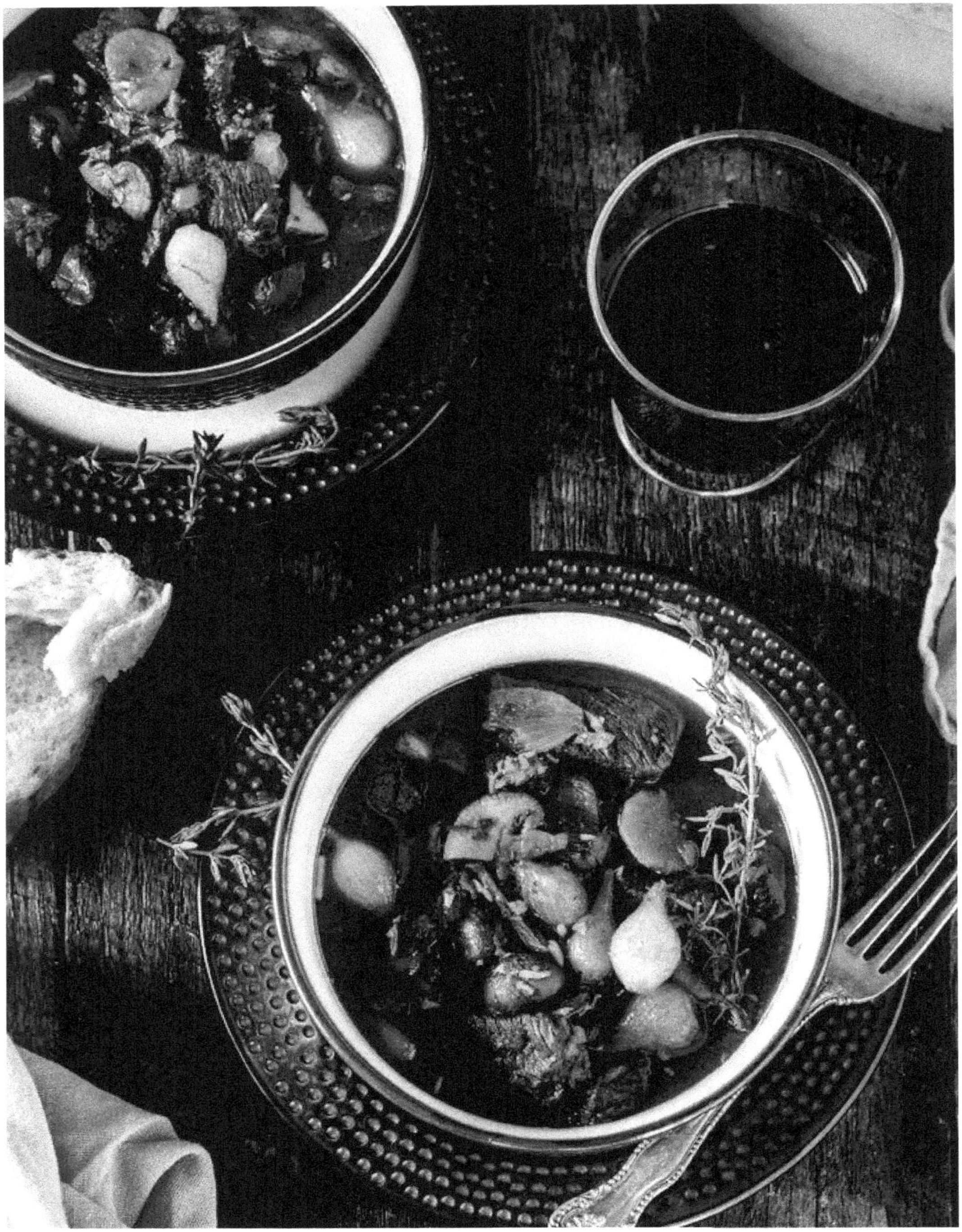

Lush Vegetable Frittata

Prep time: 15 minutes | Cook time: 20 minutes | Serves 2

- 4 eggs
- 1/3 cup milk
- 2 teaspoons olive oil
- 1 large zucchini, sliced
- 2 asparagus, sliced thinly
- 1/3 cup sliced mushrooms
- 1 cup baby spinach
- 1 small red onion, sliced
- 1/3 cup crumbled feta cheese
- 1/3 cup grated Cheddar cheese
- ¼ cup chopped chives
- Salt and ground black pepper, to taste

1. Line a baking pan with parchment paper.
2. Whisk together the eggs, salt, ground black pepper, and milk in a large bowl. Set aside.
3. Heat the olive oil in a nonstick skillet over medium heat until shimmering.
4. Add the mushrooms, zucchini, spinach, asparagus, and onion to the skillet and sauté for 5 minutes or until tender.
5. Pour the sautéed vegetables into the prepared baking pan, then spread the egg mixture over and scatter with cheeses.
6. Place the pan on the bake position.
7. Select Bake, set temperature to 380ºF (193ºC) and set time to 15 minutes. Stir the mixture halfway through.
8. When cooking is complete, the egg should be set and the edges should be lightly browned.
9. Remove the frittata from the air fryer grill and sprinkle with chives before serving.

Burgundy Steak and Mushroom Casserole

Prep time: 10 minutes | Cook time: 25 minutes | Serves 4

- 1½ pounds (680 g) beef steak
- 1 ounce (28 g) dry onion soup mix
- 2 cups sliced mushrooms
- 1 (14.5-ounce / 411-g) can cream of mushroom soup
- ½ cup beef broth
- ¼ cup red wine
- 3 garlic cloves, minced
- 1 whole onion, chopped

1. Put the beef steak in a large bowl, then sprinkle with dry onion soup mix. Toss to coat well.
2. Combine the mushrooms with garlic, onion, beef broth, mushroom soup, and red wine in a large bowl. Stir to mix well.

3. Transfer the beef steak in a baking pan, then pour in the mushroom mixture.
4. Place the pan on the bake position.
5. Select Bake, set temperature to 360ºF (182ºC) and set time to 25 minutes.
6. When cooking is complete, the mushrooms should be soft and the beef should be well browned.
7. Remove the baking pan from the air fryer grill and serve immediately.

Fast Chicken Sausage and Broccoli Casserole

Prep time: 10 minutes | Cook time: 20 minutes | Serves 8

- 10 eggs
- 1 cup Cheddar cheese, shredded and divided
- ¾ cup heavy whipping cream
- 1 (12-ounce / 340-g) package cooked chicken sausage
- 1 cup broccoli, chopped
- 2 cloves garlic, minced
- ½ tablespoon salt
- ¼ tablespoon ground black pepper
- Cooking spray

1. Spritz a baking pan with cooking spray.
2. Whisk the eggs with Cheddar and cream in a large bowl to mix well.
3. Combine the garlic, broccoli, cooked sausage, salt, and ground black pepper in a separate bowl. Stir to mix well.
4. Pour the sausage mixture into the baking pan, then spread the egg mixture over to cover.
5. Place the pan on the bake position.
6. Select Bake, set temperature to 400ºF (205ºC) and set time to 20 minutes.
7. When cooking is complete, the egg should be set and a toothpick inserted in the center should come out clean.
8. Serve immediately.

Cheesy Keto Quiche

Prep time: 20 minutes | Cook time: 1 hour | Serves 8

Crust:
- 1¼ cups blanched almond flour
- 1 large egg, beaten
- 1¼ cups grated Parmesan cheese
- ¼ teaspoon fine sea salt

Filling:
- 4 ounces (113 g) cream cheese
- 1 cup shredded Swiss cheese
- ⅓ cup minced leeks
- 4 large eggs, beaten
- ½ cup chicken broth
- ⅛ teaspoon cayenne pepper
- ¾ teaspoon fine sea salt
- 1 tablespoon unsalted butter, melted
- Chopped green onions, for garnish
- Cooking spray

1. Spritz a pie pan with cooking spray.
2. Combine the egg, flour, salt, and Parmesan in a large bowl. Stir to mix until a satiny and firm dough forms.
3. Arrange the dough between two grease parchment papers, then roll the dough into a 1/16-inch thick circle.
4. Make the crust: Transfer the dough into the prepared pie pan and press to coat the bottom.
5. Place the pan on the bake position.
6. Select Bake, set temperature to 325ºF (163ºC) and set time to 12 minutes.
7. When cooking is complete, the edges of the crust should be lightly browned.
8. Meanwhile, combine the ingredient for the filling, except for the green onions in a large bowl.
9. Pour the filling over the cooked crust and cover the edges of the crust with aluminum foil.
10. Place the pan on the bake position.
11. Select Bake. Set time to 15 minutes.
12. When cooking is complete, reduce the heat to 300ºF (150ºC) and set time to 30 minutes.
13. When cooking is complete, a toothpick inserted in the center should come out clean.
14. Remove the pie pan from the air fryer grill and allow to cool for 10 minutes before serving.

Hearty Pimento and Almond Turkey Casserole

Prep time: 5 minutes | Cook time: 32 minutes | Serves 4

- 1 pound (454 g) turkey breasts
- 1 tablespoon olive oil
- 2 boiled eggs, chopped
- 2 tablespoons chopped pimentos
- ¼ cup slivered almonds, chopped
- ¼ cup mayonnaise
- ½ cup diced celery
- 2 tablespoons chopped green onion
- ¼ cup cream of chicken soup
- ¼ cup bread crumbs
- Salt and ground black pepper, to taste

1. Put the turkey breasts in a large bowl. Sprinkle with salt and ground black pepper and drizzle with olive oil. Toss to coat well.
2. Transfer the turkey in the air fry basket.
3. Place the basket on the air fry position.
4. Select Air Fry. Set temperature to 390°F (199°C) and set time to 12 minutes. Flip the turkey halfway through.
5. When cooking is complete, the turkey should be well browned.
6. Remove the turkey breasts from the air fryer grill and cut into cubes, then combine the chicken cubes with eggs, almonds, green onions, pimentos, celery, mayo, and chicken soup in a large bowl. Stir to mix.
7. Pour the mixture into a baking pan, then spread with bread crumbs.
8. Place the pan on the bake position.
9. Select Bake. Set time to 20 minutes.
10. When cooking is complete, the eggs should be set.
11. Remove the baking pan from the air fryer grill and serve immediately.

Chapter 11

Wraps and Sandwiches

- 85　Pork Wonton
- 85　Crunchy Chicken Egg Rolls
- 86　Golden Chicken and Yogurt Taquitos
- 87　Spinach and Ricotta Pockets
- 88　Crunchy Shrimp and Zucchini Potstickers

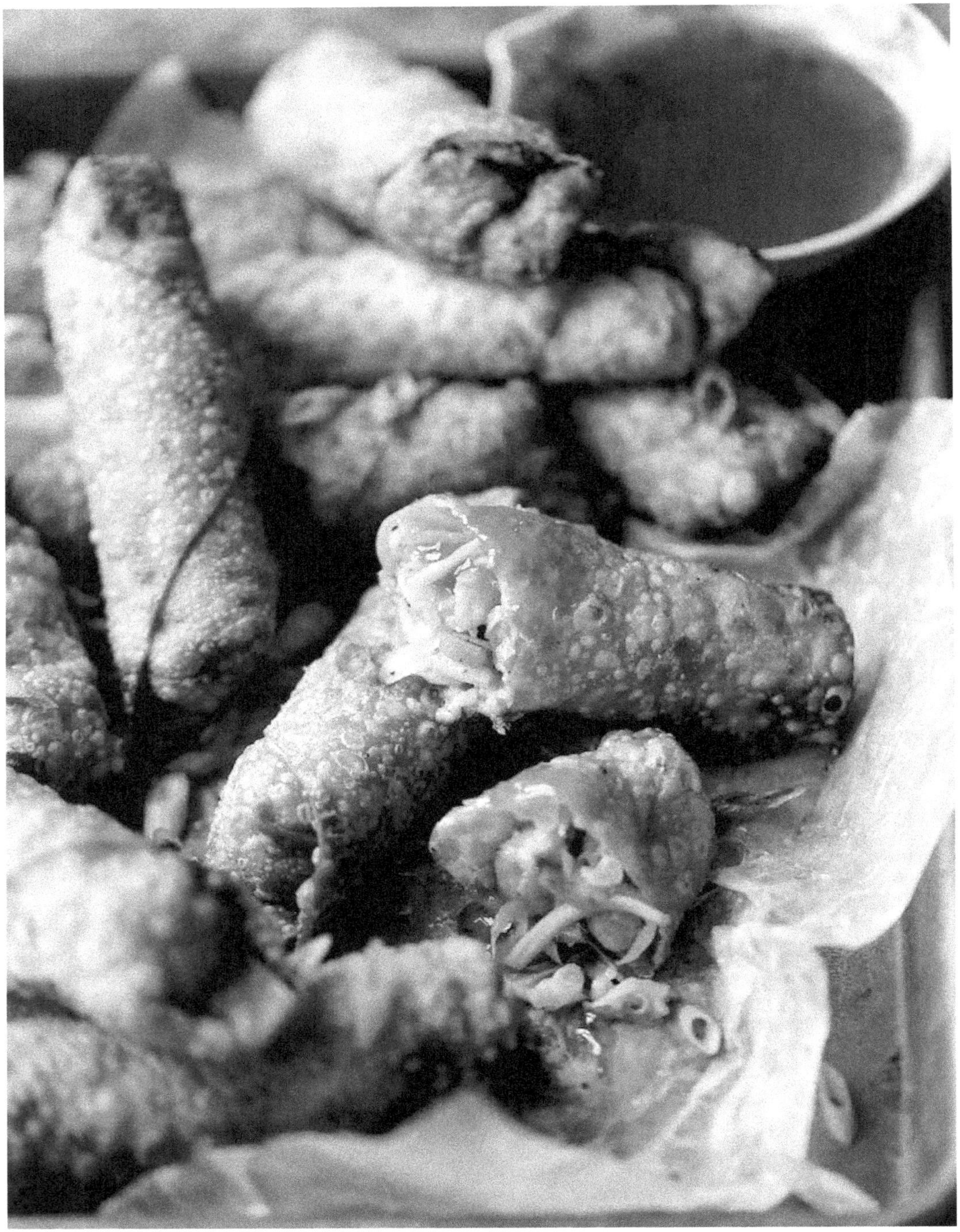

Pork Wonton

Prep time: 20 minutes | Cook time: 20 minutes | Serves 4

- 2 tablespoons olive oil
- 1 pound (454 g) ground pork
- 1 shredded carrot
- 1 onion, chopped
- 1 teaspoon soy sauce
- 16 wonton wrappers
- Salt and ground black pepper, to taste
- Cooking spray

1. Heat the olive oil in a nonstick skillet over medium heat until shimmering.
2. Add the ground pork, onion, carrot, salt, ground black pepper, and soy sauce and sauté for 10 minutes or until the pork is well browned and carrots are tender.
3. Unfold the wrappers on a clean work surface, then divide the cooked pork and vegetables on the wrappers. Fold the edges around the filling to form momos. Nip the top to seal the momos.
4. Arrange the momos in the air fry basket and spritz with cooking spray.
5. Place the basket on the air fry position.
6. Select Air Fry, set temperature to 320ºF (160ºC) and set time to 10 minutes.
7. When cooking is complete, the wrappers will be lightly browned.
8. Serve immediately.

Crunchy Chicken Egg Rolls

Prep time: 10 minutes | Cook time: 23 to 24 minutes | Serves 4

- 1 pound (454 g) ground chicken
- 2 teaspoons olive oil
- 2 garlic cloves, minced
- 1 teaspoon grated fresh ginger
- 2 cups white cabbage, shredded
- 1 onion, chopped
- ¼ cup soy sauce
- 8 egg roll wrappers
- 1 egg, beaten
- Cooking spray

1. Spritz the air fry basket with cooking spray.
2. Heat olive oil in a saucepan over medium heat. Sauté the garlic and ginger in the olive oil for 1 minute, or until fragrant. Add the ground chicken to the saucepan. Sauté for 5 minutes, or until the chicken is cooked through. Add the cabbage, onion and soy sauce and sauté for 5 to 6 minutes, or until the vegetables become soft. Remove the saucepan from the heat.

Wraps and Sandwiches

3. Unfold the egg roll wrappers on a clean work surface. Divide the chicken mixture among the wrappers and brush the edges of the wrappers with the beaten egg. Tightly roll up the egg rolls, enclosing the filling. Arrange the rolls in the basket.
4. Place the basket on the air fry position.
5. Select Air Fry, set temperature to 370ºF (188ºC) and set time to 12 minutes. Flip the rolls halfway through the cooking time.
6. When cooked, the rolls will be crispy and golden brown.
7. Transfer to a platter and let cool for 5 minutes before serving.

Golden Chicken and Yogurt Taquitos

Prep time: 15 minutes | Cook time: 12 minutes | Serves 4

- 1 cup cooked chicken, shredded
- ¼ cup Greek yogurt
- ¼ cup salsa
- 1 cup shredded Mozzarella cheese
- Salt and ground black pepper, to taste
- 4 flour tortillas
- Cooking spray

1. Spritz the air fry basket with cooking spray.
2. Combine all the ingredients, except for the tortillas, in a large bowl. Stir to mix well.
3. Make the taquitos: Unfold the tortillas on a clean work surface, then scoop up 2 tablespoons of the chicken mixture in the middle of each tortilla. Roll the tortillas up to wrap the filling.
4. Arrange the taquitos in the basket and spritz with cooking spray.
5. Place the basket on the air fry position.
6. Select Air Fry, set temperature to 380ºF (193ºC) and set time to 12 minutes. Flip the taquitos halfway through the cooking time.
7. When cooked, the taquitos should be golden brown and the cheese should be melted.
8. Serve immediately.

Spinach and Ricotta Pockets

Prep time: 20 minutes | Cook time: 10 minutes | Makes 8 pockets

- 2 large eggs, divided
- 1 tablespoon water
- 1 cup baby spinach, roughly chopped
- ¼ cup sun-dried tomatoes, finely chopped
- 1 cup ricotta cheese
- 1 cup basil, chopped
- ¼ teaspoon red pepper flakes
- ¼ teaspoon kosher salt
- 2 refrigerated rolled pie crusts
- 2 tablespoons sesame seeds

1. Spritz the air fry basket with cooking spray.
2. Whisk an egg with water in a small bowl.
3. Combine the tomatoes, spinach, the other egg, basil, ricotta cheese, salt, and red pepper flakes in a large bowl. Whisk to mix well.
4. Unfold the pie crusts on a clean work surface and slice each crust into 4 wedges. Scoop up 3 tablespoons of the spinach mixture on each crust and leave ½ inch space from edges.
5. Fold the crust wedges in half to wrap the filling and press the edges with a fork to seal.
6. Arrange the wraps in the basket and spritz with cooking spray. Sprinkle with sesame seeds.
7. Place the basket on the air fry position.
8. Select Air Fry, set temperature to 380ºF (193ºC) and set time to 10 minutes. Flip the wraps halfway through the cooking time.
9. When cooked, the wraps will be crispy and golden.
10. Serve immediately.

Crunchy Shrimp and Zucchini Potstickers

Prep time: 35 minutes | Cook time: 5 minutes | Serves 10

- ½ pound (227 g) peeled and deveined shrimp, finely chopped
- 1 medium zucchini, coarsely grated
- 1 tablespoon fish sauce
- 1 tablespoon green curry paste
- 2 scallions, thinly sliced
- ¼ cup basil, chopped
- 30 round dumpling wrappers
- Cooking spray

1. Combine the zucchini, chopped shrimp, curry paste, fish sauce, basil, and scallions in a large bowl. Stir to mix well.
2. Unfold the dumpling wrappers on a clean work surface, dab a little water around the edges of each wrapper, then scoop up 1 teaspoon of filling in the middle of each wrapper.
3. Make the potstickers: Fold the wrappers in half and press the edges to seal.
4. Spritz the air fry basket with cooking spray.
5. Transfer the potstickers to the basket and spritz with cooking spray.
6. Place the basket on the air fry position.
7. Select Air Fry, set temperature to 350°F (180°C) and set time to 5 minutes. Flip the potstickers halfway through the cooking time.
8. When cooking is complete, the potstickers should be crunchy and lightly browned.
9. Serve immediately.

Chapter 12

Holiday Specials

91	Crispy Arancini
92	Golden Kale Salad Sushi Rolls
93	Golden Garlicky Olive Stromboli
94	Simple Chocolate Buttermilk Cake
94	Blistered Cherry Tomatoes
95	Easy Butter Cake
95	Golden Chocolate and Coconut Macaroons
96	Fast Teriyaki Shrimp Skewers

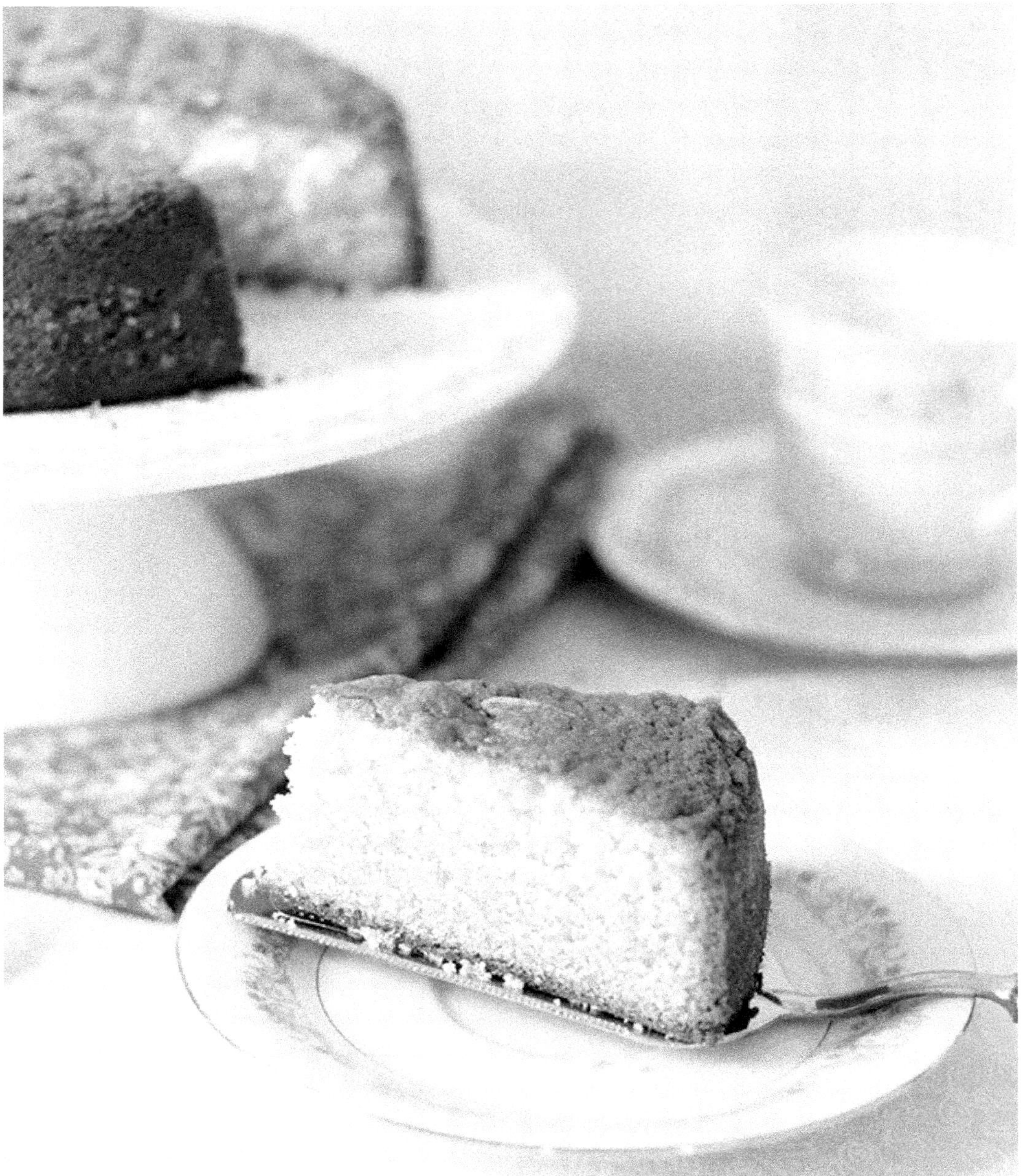

Crispy Arancini

Prep time: 5 minutes | Cook time: 30 minutes | Makes 10 arancini

- ²⁄₃ cup raw white Arborio rice
- 2 teaspoons butter
- ½ teaspoon salt
- 1 ¹⁄₃ cups water
- 2 large eggs, well beaten
- 1 ¼ cups seasoned Italian-style dried bread crumbs
- 10 ¾-inch semi-firm Mozzarella cubes
- Cooking spray

1. Pour the rice, salt, butter, and water in a pot. Stir to mix well and bring a boil over medium-high heat. Keep stirring.
2. Reduce the heat to low and cover the pot. Simmer for 20 minutes or until the rice is tender.
3. Turn off the heat and let sit, covered, for 10 minutes, then open the lid and fluffy the rice with a fork. Allow to cool for 10 more minutes.
4. Pour the beaten eggs in a bowl, then pour the bread crumbs in a separate bowl.
5. Scoop 2 tablespoons of the cooked rice up and form it into a ball, then press the Mozzarella into the ball and wrap.
6. Dredge the ball in the eggs first, then shake the excess off the dunk the ball in the bread crumbs. Roll to coat evenly. Repeat to make 10 balls in total with remaining rice.
7. Transfer the balls in the air fry basket and spritz with cooking spray.
8. Place the basket on the air fry position.
9. Select Air Fry, set temperature to 375ºF (190ºC) and set time to 10 minutes.
10. When cooking is complete, the balls should be lightly browned and crispy.
11. Remove the balls from the air fryer grill and allow to cool before serving.

Golden Kale Salad Sushi Rolls

Prep time: 10 minutes | Cook time: 10 minutes | Serves 12

Kale Salad:
- 1½ cups chopped kale
- 1 tablespoon sesame seeds
- ¾ teaspoon soy sauce
- ¾ teaspoon toasted sesame oil
- ½ teaspoon rice vinegar
- ¼ teaspoon ginger
- ⅛ teaspoon garlic powder

Sushi Rolls:
- 3 sheets sushi nori
- 1 batch cauliflower rice
- ½ avocado, sliced

Coating:
- ½ cup panko bread crumbs

- Sriracha Mayonnaise:
- ¼ cup Sriracha sauce
- ¼ cup vegan mayonnaise

1. In a medium bowl, toss all the ingredients for the salad together until well coated and set aside.
2. Place a sheet of nori on a clean work surface and spread the cauliflower rice in an even layer on the nori. Scoop 2 to 3 tablespoon of kale salad on the rice and spread over. Place 1 or 2 avocado slices on top. Roll up the sushi, pressing gently to get a nice, tight roll. Repeat to make the remaining 2 rolls.
3. In a bowl, stir together the mayonnaise and Sriracha sauce until smooth. Add bread crumbs to a separate bowl.
4. Dredge the sushi rolls in Sriracha Mayonnaise, then roll in bread crumbs till well coated.
5. Place the coated sushi rolls in the air fry basket.
6. Place the basket on the air fry position.
7. Select Air Fry, set temperature to 390ºF (199ºC) and set time to 10 minutes. Flip the sushi rolls halfway through the cooking time.
8. When cooking is complete, the sushi rolls will be golden brown and crispy.
9. Transfer to a platter and rest for 5 minutes before slicing each roll into 8 pieces. Serve warm.

Golden Garlicky Olive Stromboli

Prep time: 25 minutes | Cook time: 25 minutes | Serves 8

- 4 large cloves garlic, unpeeled
- 3 tablespoons grated Parmesan cheese
- ½ cup packed fresh basil leaves
- ½ cup marinated, pitted green and black olives
- ¼ teaspoon crushed red pepper
- ½ pound (227 g) pizza dough, at room temperature
- 4 ounces (113 g) sliced provolone cheese (about 8 slices)
- Cooking spray

1. Spritz the air fry basket with cooking spray. Put the unpeeled garlic in the air fry basket.
2. Place the basket on the air fry position.
3. Select Air Fry, set temperature to 370ºF (188ºC) and set time to 10 minutes.
4. When cooked, the garlic will be softened completely. Remove from the air fryer grill and allow to cool until you can handle.
5. Peel the garlic and place into a food processor with 2 tablespoons of basil, crushed red pepper, Parmesan, and olives. Pulse to mix well. Set aside.
6. Arrange the pizza dough on a clean work surface, then roll it out with a rolling pin into a rectangle. Cut the rectangle in half.
7. Sprinkle half of the garlic mixture over each rectangle half, and leave ½-inch edges uncover. Top them with the provolone cheese.
8. Brush one long side of each rectangle half with water, then roll them up. Spritz the air fry basket with cooking spray. Transfer the rolls to the air fry basket. Spritz with cooking spray and scatter with remaining Parmesan.
9. Place the basket on the air fry position.
10. Select Air Fry and set time to 15 minutes. Flip the rolls halfway through the cooking time. When done, the rolls should be golden brown.
11. Remove the rolls from the air fryer grill and allow to cool for a few minutes before serving.

Simple Chocolate Buttermilk Cake

Prep time: 20 minutes | Cook time: 20 minutes | Serves 8

- 1 cup all-purpose flour
- ⅔ cup granulated white sugar
- ¼ cup unsweetened cocoa powder
- ¾ teaspoon baking soda
- ¼ teaspoon salt
- ⅔ cup buttermilk
- 2 tablespoons plus 2 teaspoons vegetable oil
- 1 teaspoon vanilla extract
- Cooking spray

1. Spritz a baking pan with cooking spray.
2. Combine the flour, cocoa powder, sugar, salt, and baking soda in a large bowl. Stir to mix well.
3. Mix in the buttermilk, vegetable oil, and vanilla. Keep stirring until it forms a grainy and thick dough.
4. Scrape the chocolate batter from the bowl and transfer to the pan, level the batter in an even layer with a spatula.
5. Place the pan on the bake position.
6. Select Bake, set temperature to 325ºF (163ºC) and set time to 20 minutes.
7. After 15 minutes, remove the pan from the air fryer grill. Check the doneness. Return the pan to the air fryer grill and continue cooking.
8. When done, a toothpick inserted in the center should come out clean.
9. Invert the cake on a cooling rack and allow to cool for 15 minutes before slicing to serve.

Blistered Cherry Tomatoes

Prep time: 5 minutes | Cook time: 10 minutes | Serves 4 to 6

- 2 pounds (907 g) cherry tomatoes
- 2 tablespoons olive oil
- 2 teaspoons balsamic vinegar
- ½ teaspoon salt
- ½ teaspoon ground black pepper

1. Toss the cherry tomatoes with olive oil in a large bowl to coat well. Pour the tomatoes in a baking pan.
2. Slide the pan into the air fryer grill.
3. Select Air Fry, set temperature to 400ºF (205ºC) and set time to 10 minutes. Stir the tomatoes halfway through the cooking time.
4. When cooking is complete, the tomatoes will be blistered and lightly wilted.
5. Transfer the blistered tomatoes to a large bowl and toss with balsamic vinegar, salt, and black pepper before serving.

Easy Butter Cake

Prep time: 25 minutes | Cook time: 20 minutes | Serves 8

- 1 cup all-purpose flour
- 1¼ teaspoons baking powder
- ¼ teaspoon salt
- ½ cup plus 1½ tablespoons granulated white sugar
- 9½ tablespoons butter, at room temperature
- 2 large eggs
- 1 large egg yolk
- 2½ tablespoons milk
- 1 teaspoon vanilla extract
- Cooking spray

1. Spritz a baking pan with cooking spray.
2. Combine the flour, salt, and baking powder in a large bowl. Stir to mix well.
3. Whip the sugar and butter in a separate bowl with a hand mixer on medium speed for 3 minutes.
4. Whip the egg yolk, eggs, milk, and vanilla extract into the sugar and butter mix with a hand mixer.
5. Pour in the flour mixture and whip with hand mixer until sanity and smooth.
6. Scrape the batter into the baking pan and level the batter with a spatula.
7. Place the pan on the bake position.
8. Select Bake, set temperature to 325°F (163°C) and set time to 20 minutes.
9. After 15 minutes, remove the pan from the air fryer grill. Check the doneness. Return the pan to the air fryer grill and continue cooking.
10. When done, a toothpick inserted in the center should come out clean.
11. Invert the cake on a cooling rack and allow to cool for 15 minutes before slicing to serve.

Golden Chocolate and Coconut Macaroons

Prep time: 10 minutes | Cook time: 8 minutes | Makes 24 macaroons

- 3 large egg whites, at room temperature
- ¼ teaspoon salt
- ¾ cup granulated white sugar
- 4½ tablespoons unsweetened cocoa powder
- 2¼ cups unsweetened shredded coconut

1. Line the air fry basket with parchment paper.
2. Whisk the egg whites with salt in a large bowl with a hand mixer on high speed until stiff peaks form.

3. Whisk in the sugar with the hand mixer on high speed until the mixture is thick. Mix in the cocoa powder and coconut.
4. Scoop 2 tablespoons of the mixture and shape the mixture in a ball. Repeat with remaining mixture to make 24 balls in total.
5. Arrange the balls in a single layer in the air fry basket and leave a little space between each two balls.
6. Place the basket on the air fry position.
7. Select Air Fry, set temperature to 375℉ (190℃) and set time to 8 minutes.
8. When cooking is complete, the balls should be golden brown.
9. Serve immediately.

Fast Teriyaki Shrimp Skewers

Prep time: 10 minutes | Cook time: 6 minutes | Makes 12 skewered shrimp

- 1½ tablespoons mirin
- 1½ teaspoons ginger juice
- 1½ tablespoons soy sauce
- 12 large shrimp (about 20 shrimps per pound), peeled and deveined
- 1 large egg
- ¾ cup panko bread crumbs
- Cooking spray

1. Combine the mirin, soy sauce, and ginger juice in a large bowl. Stir to mix well.
2. Dunk the shrimp in the bowl of mirin mixture, then wrap the bowl in plastic and refrigerate for 1 hour to marinate.
3. Spritz the air fry basket with cooking spray.
4. Run twelve 4-inch skewers through each shrimp.
5. Whisk the egg in the bowl of marinade to combine well. Pour the bread crumbs on a plate.
6. Dredge the shrimp skewers in the egg mixture, then shake the excess off and roll over the bread crumbs to coat well.
7. Arrange the shrimp skewers in the air fry basket and spritz with cooking spray.
8. Place the basket on the air fry position.
9. Select Air Fry, set temperature to 400℉ (205℃) and set time to 6 minutes. Flip the shrimp skewers halfway through the cooking time.
10. When done, the shrimp will be opaque and firm.
11. Serve immediately.

Chapter 13

Fast and Easy Everyday Favorites

- 99   Fast Traditional Latkes
- 99   Fast Baked Cherry Tomatoes
- 100   Crispy Brussels Sprouts
- 100   Crunchy Salty Tortilla Chips
- 101   Crunchy Sweet Cinnamon Chickpeas
- 101   Panko Salmon and Carrot Croquettes
- 102   Air-Fried Squash with Hazelnuts
- 102   Spicy Chicken Wings
- 103   Golden Bacon Pinwheels

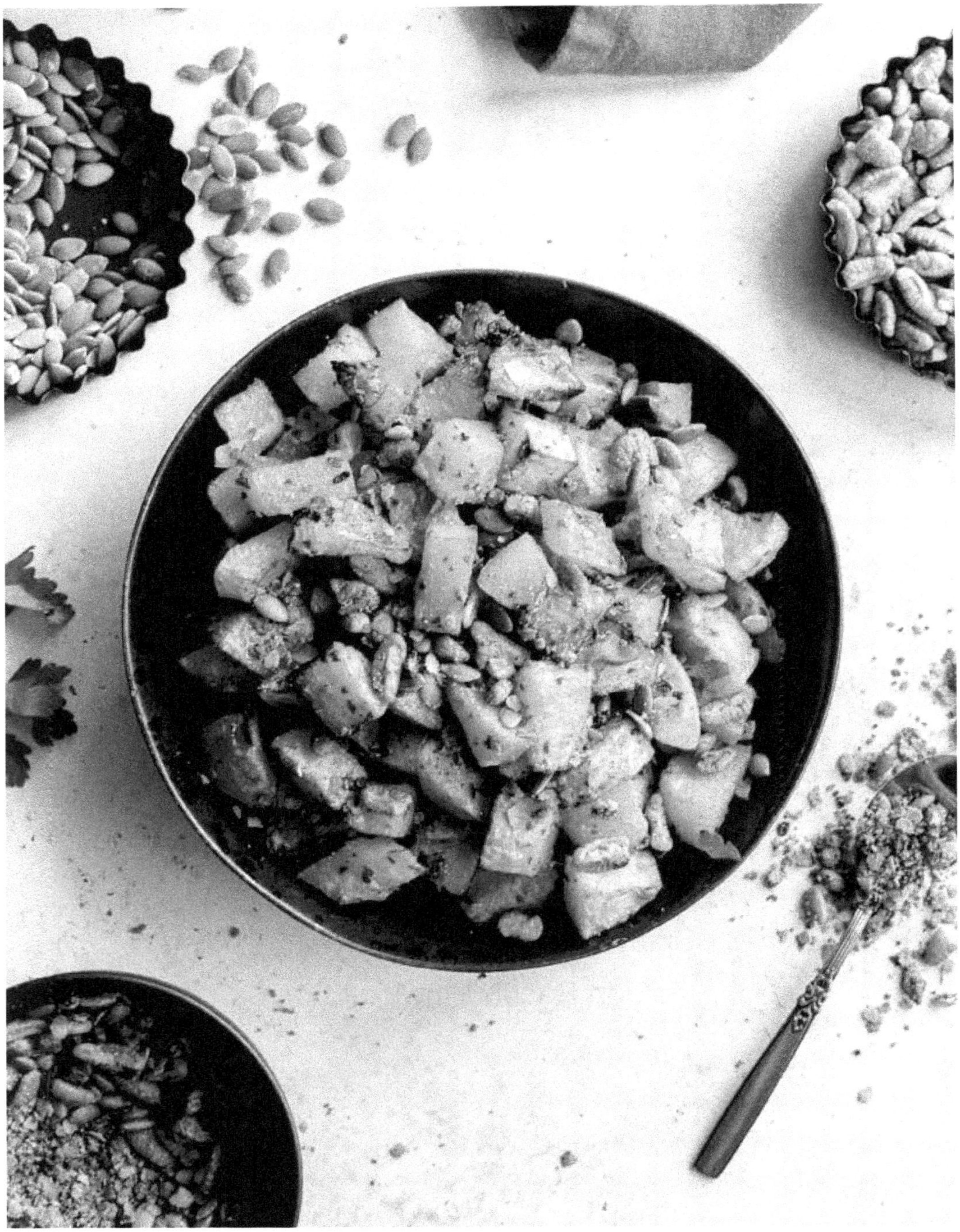

Fast Traditional Latkes

Prep time: 15 minutes | Cook time: 10 minutes | Makes 4 latkes

- 1 egg
- 2 tablespoons all-purpose flour
- 2 medium potatoes, peeled and shredded, rinsed and drained
- ¼ teaspoon granulated garlic
- ½ teaspoon salt
- Cooking spray

1. Spritz the air fry basket with cooking spray.
2. Whisk together the egg, flour, potatoes, garlic, and salt in a large bowl. Stir to mix well.
3. Divide the mixture into four parts, then flatten them into four circles. Arrange the circles onto the air fry basket and spritz with cooking spray.
4. Place the basket on the air fry position.
5. Select Air Fry, set temperature to 380ºF (193ºC) and set time to 10 minutes. Flip the latkes halfway through.
6. When cooked, the latkes will be golden brown and crispy. Remove the basket from the air fryer grill.
7. Serve immediately.

Fast Baked Cherry Tomatoes

Prep time: 5 minutes | Cook time: 5 minutes | Serves 2

- 2 cups cherry tomatoes
- 1 clove garlic, thinly sliced
- 1 teaspoon olive oil
- ⅛ teaspoon kosher salt
- 1 tablespoon freshly chopped basil, for topping
- Cooking spray

1. Spritz a baking pan with cooking spray and set aside.
2. In a large bowl, toss together the cherry tomatoes, sliced garlic, olive oil, and kosher salt. Spread the mixture in an even layer in the prepared pan.
3. Place the pan on the bake position.
4. Select Bake, set temperature to 360ºF (182ºC) and set time to 5 minutes.
5. When cooking is complete, the tomatoes should be the soft and wilted.
6. Transfer to a bowl and rest for 5 minutes. Top with the chopped basil and serve warm.

Crispy Brussels Sprouts

Prep time: 5 minutes | Cook time: 20 minutes | Serves 4

- ¼ teaspoon salt
- ⅛ teaspoon ground black pepper
- 1 tablespoon extra-virgin olive oil
- 1 pound (454 g) Brussels sprouts, trimmed and halved
- Lemon wedges, for garnish

1. Combine the olive oil, salt, and black pepper in a large bowl. Stir to mix well.
2. Add the Brussels sprouts to the bowl of mixture and toss to coat well. Arrange the Brussels sprouts in the air fry basket.
3. Place the basket on the air fry position.
4. Select Air Fry, set temperature to 350ºF (180ºC) and set time to 20 minutes. Stir the Brussels sprouts two times during cooking.
5. When cooked, the Brussels sprouts will be lightly browned and wilted. Remove from the air fryer grill.
6. Transfer the cooked Brussels sprouts to a large plate and squeeze the lemon wedges on top to serve.

Crunchy Salty Tortilla Chips

Prep time: 5 minutes | Cook time: 10 minutes | Serves 4

- 4 six-inch corn tortillas, cut in half and slice into thirds
- 1 tablespoon canola oil
- ¼ teaspoon kosher salt
- Cooking spray

1. Spritz the air fry basket with cooking spray.
2. On a clean work surface, brush the tortilla chips with canola oil, then transfer the chips to the air fry basket.
3. Place the basket on the air fry position.
4. Select Air Fry, set temperature to 360ºF (182ºC) and set time to 10 minutes. Flip the chips and sprinkle with salt halfway through the cooking time.
5. When cooked, the chips will be crunchy and lightly browned. Transfer the chips to a plate lined with paper towels. Serve immediately.

Crunchy Sweet Cinnamon Chickpeas

Prep time: 10 minutes | Cook time: 10 minutes | Serves 2

- 1 tablespoon cinnamon
- 1 tablespoon sugar
- 1 cup chickpeas, soaked in water overnight, rinsed and drained

1. Combine the cinnamon and sugar in a bowl. Stir to mix well.
2. Add the chickpeas to the bowl, then toss to coat well.
3. Pour the chickpeas in the air fry basket.
4. Place the basket on the air fry position.
5. Select Air Fry, set temperature to 390ºF (199ºC) and set time to 10 minutes. Stir the chickpeas three times during cooking.
6. When cooked, the chickpeas should be golden brown and crispy. Remove the basket from the air fryer grill.
7. Serve immediately.

Panko Salmon and Carrot Croquettes

Prep time: 15 minutes | Cook time: 10 minutes | Serves 6

- 2 egg whites
- 1 cup almond flour
- 1 cup panko bread crumbs
- 1 pound (454 g) chopped salmon fillet
- 2/3 cup grated carrots
- 2 tablespoons minced garlic cloves
- ½ cup chopped onion
- 2 tablespoons chopped chives
- Cooking spray

1. Spritz the air fry basket with cooking spray.
2. Whisk the egg whites in a bowl. Put the flour in a second bowl. Pour the bread crumbs in a third bowl. Set aside.
3. Combine the salmon, garlic, onion, carrots, and chives in a large bowl. Stir to mix well.
4. Form the mixture into balls with your hands. Dredge the balls into the flour, then egg, and then bread crumbs to coat well.
5. Arrange the salmon balls in the air fry basket and spritz with cooking spray.
6. Place the basket on the air fry position.
7. Select Air Fry, set temperature to 350ºF (180ºC) and set time to 10 minutes. Flip the salmon balls halfway through cooking.
8. When cooking is complete, the salmon balls will be crispy and browned. Remove the basket from the air fryer grill.
9. Serve immediately.

Air-Fried Squash with Hazelnuts

Prep time: 10 minutes | Cook time: 23 minutes | Makes 3 cups

- 2 tablespoons whole hazelnuts
- 3 cups butternut squash, peeled, deseeded and cubed
- ¼ teaspoon kosher salt
- ¼ teaspoon freshly ground black pepper
- 2 teaspoons olive oil
- Cooking spray

1. Spritz the air fry basket with cooking spray. Spread the hazelnuts in the basket.
2. Place the basket on the air fry position.
3. Select Air Fry, set temperature to 300ºF (150ºC) and set time to 3 minutes.
4. When done, the hazelnuts should be soft. Remove from the air fryer grill. Chopped the hazelnuts roughly and transfer to a small bowl. Set aside.
5. Put the butternut squash in a large bowl, then sprinkle with salt and pepper and drizzle with olive oil. Toss to coat well. Transfer the squash to the lightly greased basket.
6. Place the basket on the air fry position.
7. Select Air Fry, set temperature to 360ºF (182ºC) and set time to 20 minutes. Flip the squash halfway through the cooking time.
8. When cooking is complete, the squash will be soft. Transfer the squash to a plate and sprinkle with the chopped hazelnuts before serving.

Spicy Chicken Wings

Prep time: 5 minutes | Cook time: 15 minutes | Makes 16 wings

- 16 chicken wings
- 3 tablespoons hot sauce
- Cooking spray

1. Spritz the air fry basket with cooking spray.
2. Arrange the chicken wings in the air fry basket.
3. Place the basket on the air fry position.
4. Select Air Fry, set temperature to 360ºF (182ºC) and set time to 15 minutes. Flip the wings at lease three times during cooking.
5. When cooking is complete, the chicken wings will be well browned. Remove the pan from the air fryer grill.
6. Transfer the air fried wings to a plate and serve with hot sauce.

Golden Bacon Pinwheels

Prep time: 5 minutes | Cook time: 10 minutes | Makes 8 pinwheels

- 1 sheet puff pastry
- 2 tablespoons maple syrup
- ¼ cup brown sugar
- 8 slices bacon
- Ground black pepper, to taste
- Cooking spray

1. Spritz the air fry basket with cooking spray.
2. Roll the puff pastry into a 10-inch square with a rolling pin on a clean work surface, then cut the pastry into 8 strips.
3. Brush the strips with maple syrup and sprinkle with sugar, leaving a 1-inch far end uncovered.
4. Arrange each slice of bacon on each strip, leaving a ⅛-inch length of bacon hang over the end close to you. Sprinkle with black pepper.
5. From the end close to you, roll the strips into pinwheels, then dab the uncovered end with water and seal the rolls.
6. Arrange the pinwheels in the air fry basket and spritz with cooking spray.
7. Place the basket on the air fry position.
8. Select Air Fry, set temperature to 360ºF (182ºC) and set time to 10 minutes. Flip the pinwheels halfway through.
9. When cooking is complete, the pinwheels should be golden brown. Remove the pan from the air fryer grill.
10. Serve immediately.

Chapter 14

Rotisserie Recipes

- **106** Air-Fried Lemony-Garlicky Chicken
- **106** Spicy-Sweet Pork Tenderloin
- **107** Apple, Carrot, and Onion Stuffed Turkey
- **108** Toasted Rotisserie Pork Shoulder

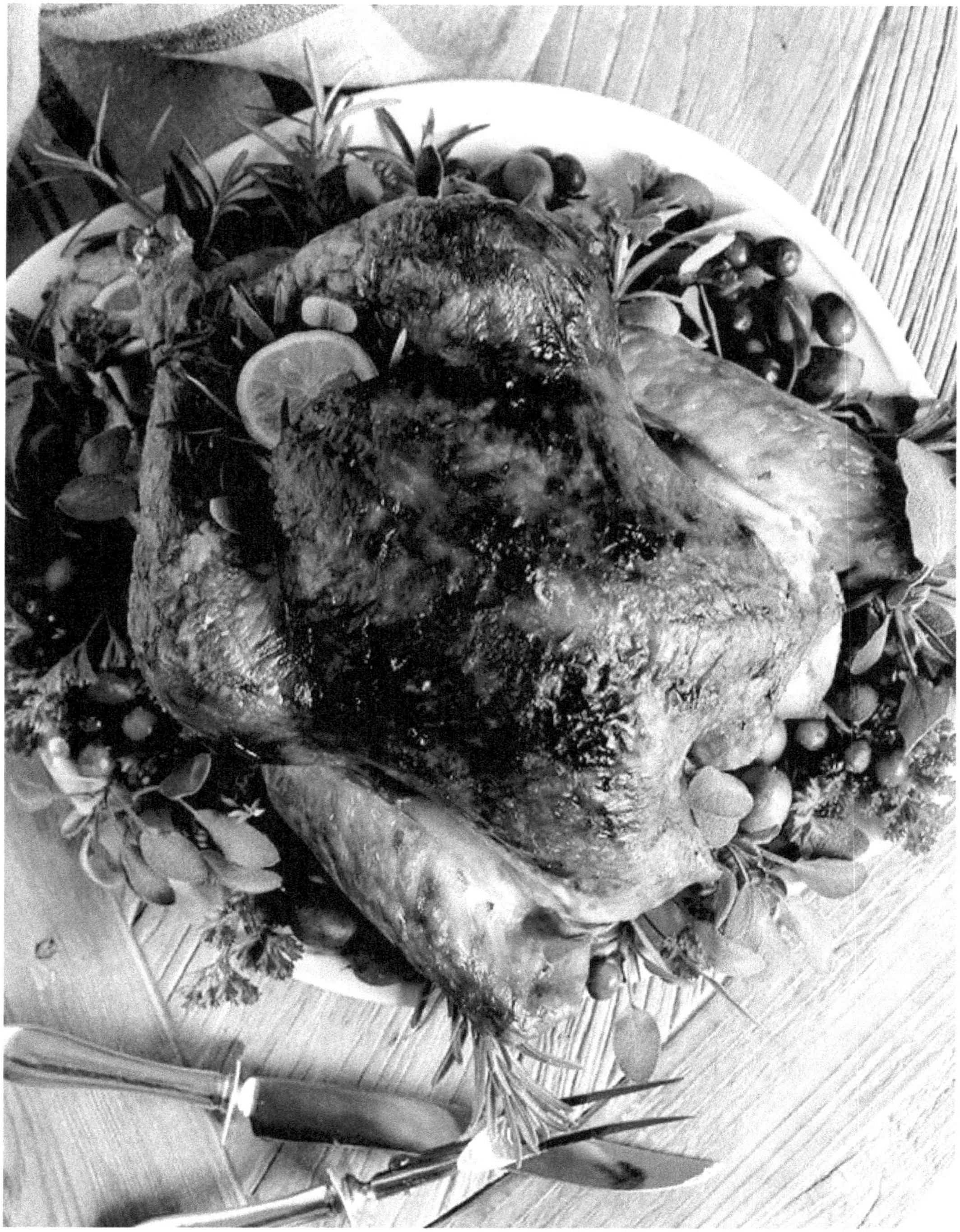

Air-Fried Lemony-Garlicky Chicken

Prep time: 10 minutes | Cook time: 45 minutes | Serves 4

- 3 pounds (1.4 kg) tied whole chicken
- 3 cloves garlic, halved
- 1 whole lemon, quartered
- 2 sprigs fresh rosemary whole
- 2 tablespoons olive oil
- Chicken Rub:
- ½ teaspoon fresh ground pepper
- ½ teaspoon salt
- 1 teaspoon garlic powder
- 1 teaspoon dried oregano
- 1 teaspoon paprika
- 1 sprig rosemary (leaves only)

1. Mix together the rub ingredients in a small bowl. Set aside.
2. Place the chicken on a clean cutting board. Ensure the cavity of the chicken is clean. Stuff the chicken cavity with the garlic, lemon, and rosemary.
3. Tie your chicken with twine if needed. Pat the chicken dry.
4. Drizzle the olive oil all over and coat the entire chicken with a brush.
5. Shake the rub on the chicken and rub in until the chicken is covered.
6. Using the rotisserie spit, push through the chicken and attach the rotisserie forks.
7. If desired, place aluminum foil onto the drip pan. (It makes for easier clean-up!)
8. Place the prepared chicken with the rotisserie spit into the air fryer grill.
9. Select Air Fry, set the temperature to 375ºF (190ºC). Set the time to 40 minutes. Check the temp in 5 minute increments after the 40 minutes.
10. At 40 minutes, check the temperature every 5 minutes until the chicken reaches 165ºF (74ºC) in the breast, or 165ºF (85ºC) in the thigh.
11. Once cooking is complete, remove the chicken using the rotisserie lift and, using hot pads or gloves, carefully remove the chicken from the spit.
12. Let the chicken sit, covered, for 5 to 10 minutes.
13. Slice and serve.

Spicy-Sweet Pork Tenderloin

Prep time: 20 minutes | Cook time: 25 minutes | Serves 2 to 3

- 1 pound (454 g) pork tenderloin
- 2 tablespoons Sriracha hot sauce
- 2 tablespoons honey
- 1½ teaspoons kosher salt

1. Stir together the honey, Sriracha hot sauce, and salt in a bowl. Rub the sauce all over the pork tenderloin.

2. Using the rotisserie spit, push through the pork tenderloin and attach the rotisserie forks.
3. If desired, place aluminum foil onto the drip pan. (It makes for easier clean-up!)
4. Place the prepared pork tenderloin with rotisserie spit into the air fryer grill.
5. Select Air Fry, set temperature to 350°F (180°C), Rotate, and set time to 20 minutes.
6. When cooking is complete, remove the pork tenderloin using the rotisserie lift and, using hot pads or gloves, carefully remove the chicken from the spit.
7. Let rest for 5 minutes and serve.

Apple, Carrot, and Onion Stuffed Turkey

Prep time: 30 minutes | Cook time: 3 hours | Serves 12 to 14

- 1 (12-pound/5.4-kg) turkey, giblet removed, rinsed and pat dry

Seasoning:
- ¼ cup lemon pepper
- 2 tablespoons chopped fresh parsley
- 1 tablespoon celery salt
- 2 cloves garlic, minced
- 2 teaspoons ground black pepper
- 1 teaspoon sage

Stuffing:
- 1 medium onion, cut into 8 equal parts
- 1 carrot, sliced
- 1 apple, cored and cut into 8 thick slices

1. Mix together the seasoning in a small bowl. Rub over the surface and inside of the turkey.
2. Stuff the turkey with the onions, carrots, and apples. Using the rotisserie spit, push through the turkey and attach the rotisserie forks.
3. If desired, place aluminum foil onto the drip pan. (It makes for easier clean-up!)
4. Place the prepared turkey with rotisserie spit into the air fryer grill
5. Select Toast, set temperature to 350°F (180°C), Rotate, and set time to 3 hours..
6. When cooking is complete, the internal temperature should read at least 180°F (82°C). Remove the lamb leg using the rotisserie lift and, using hot pads or gloves, carefully remove the turkey from the spit.
7. Server hot.

Toasted Rotisserie Pork Shoulder

Prep time: 30 minutes | Cook time: 4 hours 30 minutes | Serves 6 to 8

- 1 (5-pound / 2.3-kg) boneless pork shoulder

Rub:
- 2 teaspoons ground black peppercorns
- 2 teaspoons ground mustard seed
- 2 tablespoons light brown sugar

Mop:
- 1 cup bourbon
- 1 small onion, granulated
- ¼ cup corn syrup

- 1 tablespoon kosher salt

- 1 teaspoon onion powder
- 1 teaspoon garlic powder
- 1 teaspoon paprika

- ¼ cup ketchup
- 2 tablespoons brown mustard
- ½ cup light brown sugar

1. Combine the ingredients for the rub in a small bowl. Stir to mix well.
2. Season pork shoulder all over with rub, wrap in plastic, and place in refrigerator for 12 to 15 hours.
3. Remove roast from the fridge and let meat stand at room temperature for 30 to 45 minutes. Season with kosher salt.
4. Whisk ingredients for mop in a medium bowl. Set aside until ready to use.
5. Using the rotisserie spit, push through the pork should and attach the rotisserie forks.
6. If desired, place aluminum foil onto the drip pan. (It makes for easier clean-up!)
7. Place the prepared pork with rotisserie spit into the air fryer grill.
8. Select Toast, set temperature to 450ºF (235ºC), Rotate, and set time to 30 minutes.
9. After 30 minutes, reduce the temperature to 250ºF (121ºC) and roast for 4 more hours or until an meat thermometer inserted in the center of the pork reads at least 145ºF (63ºC).
10. After the first hour of cooking, apply mop over the pork for every 20 minutes.
11. When cooking is complete, remove the pork using the rotisserie lift and, using hot pads or gloves, carefully remove the pork tenderloin from the spit.
12. Let stand for 10 minutes before slicing and serving.

Appendix 1: Measurement Conversion Chart

VOLUME EQUIVALENTS(DRY)

US STANDARD	METRIC (APPROXIMATE)
1/8 teaspoon	0.5 mL
1/4 teaspoon	1 mL
1/2 teaspoon	2 mL
3/4 teaspoon	4 mL
1 teaspoon	5 mL
1 tablespoon	15 mL
1/4 cup	59 mL
1/2 cup	118 mL
3/4 cup	177 mL
1 cup	235 mL
2 cups	475 mL
3 cups	700 mL
4 cups	1 L

WEIGHT EQUIVALENTS

US STANDARD	METRIC (APPROXIMATE)
1 ounce	28 g
2 ounces	57 g
5 ounces	142 g
10 ounces	284 g
15 ounces	425 g
16 ounces (1 pound)	455 g
1.5 pounds	680 g
2 pounds	907 g

VOLUME EQUIVALENTS(LIQUID)

US STANDARD	US STANDARD (OUNCES)	METRIC (APPROXIMATE)
2 tablespoons	1 fl.oz.	30 mL
1/4 cup	2 fl.oz.	60 mL
1/2 cup	4 fl.oz.	120 mL
1 cup	8 fl.oz.	240 mL
1 1/2 cup	12 fl.oz.	355 mL
2 cups or 1 pint	16 fl.oz.	475 mL
4 cups or 1 quart	32 fl.oz.	1 L
1 gallon	128 fl.oz.	4 L

TEMPERATURES EQUIVALENTS

FAHRENHEIT(F)	CELSIUS(C) (APPROXIMATE)
225 °F	107 °C
250 °F	120 °C
275 °F	135 °C
300 °F	150 °C
325 °F	160 °C
350 °F	180 °C
375 °F	190 °C
400 °F	205 °C
425 °F	220 °C
450 °F	235 °C
475 °F	245 °C
500 °F	260 °C

Appendix 2 Air Fryer Cooking Chart

Beef

Item	Temp (°F)	Time (mins)	Item	Temp (°F)	Time (mins)
Beef Eye Round Roast (4 lbs.)	400 °F	45 to 55	Meatballs (1-inch)	370 °F	7
Burger Patty (4 oz.)	370 °F	16 to 20	Meatballs (3-inch)	380 °F	10
Filet Mignon (8 oz.)	400 °F	18	Ribeye, bone-in (1-inch, 8 oz)	400 °F	10 to 15
Flank Steak (1.5 lbs.)	400 °F	12	Sirloin steaks (1-inch, 12 oz)	400 °F	9 to 14
Flank Steak (2 lbs.)	400 °F	20 to 28			

Chicken

Item	Temp (°F)	Time (mins)	Item	Temp (°F)	Time (mins)
Breasts, bone in (1 ¼ lb.)	370 °F	25	Legs, bone-in (1 ¾ lb.)	380 °F	30
Breasts, boneless (4 oz)	380 °F	12	Thighs, boneless (1 ½ lb.)	380 °F	18 to 20
Drumsticks (2 ½ lb.)	370 °F	20	Wings (2 lb.)	400 °F	12
Game Hen (halved 2 lb.)	390 °F	20	Whole Chicken	360 °F	75
Thighs, bone-in (2 lb.)	380 °F	22	Tenders	360 °F	8 to 10

Pork & Lamb

Item	Temp (°F)	Time (mins)	Item	Temp (°F)	Time (mins)
Bacon (regular)	400 °F	5 to 7	Pork Tenderloin	370 °F	15
Bacon (thick cut)	400 °F	6 to 10	Sausages	380 °F	15
Pork Loin (2 lb.)	360 °F	55	Lamb Loin Chops (1-inch thick)	400 °F	8 to 12
Pork Chops, bone in (1-inch, 6.5 oz)	400 °F	12	Rack of Lamb (1.5 – 2 lb.)	380 °F	22

Fish & Seafood

Item	Temp (°F)	Time (mins)	Item	Temp (°F)	Time (mins)
Calamari (8 oz)	400 °F	4	Tuna Steak	400 °F	7 to 10
Fish Fillet (1-inch, 8 oz)	400 °F	10	Scallops	400 °F	5 to 7
Salmon, fillet (6 oz)	380 °F	12	Shrimp	400 °F	5
Swordfish steak	400 °F	10			

Vegetables

INGREDIENT	AMOUNT	PREPARATION	OIL	TEMP	COOK TIME
Asparagus	2 bunches	Cut in half, trim stems	2 Tbsp	420°F	12-15 mins
Beets	1½ lbs	Peel, cut in ½-inch cubes	1 Tbsp	390°F	28-30 mins
Bell peppers (for roasting)	4 peppers	Cut in quarters, remove seeds	1 Tbsp	400°F	15-20 mins
Broccoli	1 large head	Cut in 1-2-inch florets	1 Tbsp	400°F	15-20 mins
Brussels sprouts	1 lb	Cut in half, remove stems	1 Tbsp	425°F	15-20 mins
Carrots	1 lb	Peel, cut in ¼-inch rounds	1 Tbsp	425°F	10-15 mins
Cauliflower	1 head	Cut in 1-2-inch florets	2 Tbsp	400°F	20-22 mins
Corn on the cob	7 ears	Whole ears, remove husks	1 Tbps	400°F	14-17 mins
Green beans	1 bag (12 oz)	Trim	1 Tbps	420°F	18-20 mins
Kale (for chips)	4 oz	Tear into pieces, remove stems	None	325°F	5-8 mins
Mushrooms	16 oz	Rinse, slice thinly	1 Tbps	390°F	25-30 mins
Potatoes, russet	1½ lbs	Cut in 1-inch wedges	1 Tbps	390°F	25-30 mins
Potatoes, russet	1 lb	Hand-cut fries, soak 30 mins in cold water, then pat dry	½-3 Tbps	400°F	25-28 mins
Potatoes, sweet	1 lb	Hand-cut fries, soak 30 mins in cold water, then pat dry	1 Tbps	400°F	25-28 mins
Zucchini	1 lb	Cut in eighths lengthwise, then cut in half	1 Tbps	400°F	15-20 mins

Appendix 3 Recipe Index

A
Air-Fried Lemony-Garlicky Chicken   106
Air-Fried Root Vegetable   57
Air-Fried Squash with Hazelnuts   102
Apple Pastry   18
Apple, Carrot, and Onion Stuffed Turkey   107
Asian-Inspired Dipping Sauce   12
Authentic Carne Asada   34
Avocado and Egg Burrito   21

B
Bacon Knots   15
Baked Grits   11
Baked Whole Chicken   44
Banana and Carrot Muffin   16
Berries with Nuts Streusel Topping   74
Blistered Cherry Tomatoes   94
Blistered Shishito Peppers with Lime Sauce   65
Blueberry Tortilla   15
Breaded Calf's Liver Strips   36
Breaded Crab Sticks with Mayo Sauce   30
Burgundy Steak and Mushroom Casserole   79
Butter-Wine Baked Salmon Steak   27

C-D
Char Siu (Chinese BBQ Pork)   41
Cheesy Chicken Cubes Pizza   45
Cheesy Keto Quiche   81
Cheesy Sausage Balls   69
Chicken Breast with Apple   17
Chicken Tenders with Mushroom Sauce   50
Classic Caesar Salad Dressing   11
Coffee Cake   76
Corned Beef and Eggs Hash   19
Crispy Arancini   91
Crispy Broccoli with Cheese   59
Crispy Brussels Sprouts   100
Crispy Halibut Fillets   28
Crispy Zucchini Rounds   64
Crunchy Chicken Egg Rolls   85
Crunchy Cinnamon Apple Chips   68
Crunchy Salty Tortilla Chips   100
Crunchy Shrimp and Zucchini Potstickers   88
Crunchy Sweet Cinnamon Chickpeas   101
Dijon Turkey Cheese Burgers   51

E
Easy Butter Cake   95
Easy China Spicy Turkey Thighs   45
Easy Ratatouille   55

F
Fast Baked Cherry Tomatoes   99
Fast Chicken Sausage and Broccoli Casserole   80
Fast Teriyaki Shrimp Skewers   96
Fast Traditional Latkes   99
French Toast Sticks with Strawberry Sauce   17
Fresh Berry Pancake   16
Fruity Sweet-Sour Snapper Fillet   25

G
Garlicky Toasted Mushrooms   70
Garlicky Veal Loin   37
Gold Salmon Patties   26
Golden Bacon Pinwheels   103
Golden Cheesy Corn Casserole   63

Golden Chicken and Yogurt Taquitos   86
Golden Chocolate and Coconut Macaroons   95
Golden Garlicky Olive Stromboli   93
Golden Kale Salad Sushi Rolls   92
Golden Okra with Chili   56
Ground Beef and Spinach Meatloaves 39

H-I
Hash Brown Casserole   19
Hearty Pimento and Almond Turkey Casserole   82
Hoisin Tuna with Jasmine Rice   30
Honey New York Strip   38
Honey-Glazed Vegetable   60
Indian Spicy Chicken Drumsticks   47

J-L
Japanese Yakitori   47
Lemony Brussels Sprouts   55
Lime Chicken Breasts with Cilantro 46
London Broil with Peanut Dipping Sauce   34
Lush Vegetable Frittata   79

M-O
Macadamia Nuts Breaded Pork Rack 38
Marmalade Balsamic Glazed Duck Breasts   46
Middle East Baklava   75
Olives, Almond, and Kale Baked Eggs   20

P
Panko Salmon and Carrot Croquettes   101
Panko-Crusted Green Beans   54
Peach and Cherry Chicken Chunks   48
Pecan-Crusted Catfish   26
Perpper-Onion Stuffed Chicken Rolls 44
Pork Wonton   85
Russet Potatoes with Yogurt and Chives   64

S
Schnitzels with Sour Cream and Dill Sauce   36
Simple Chocolate Buttermilk Cake   94
Smoked Paprika Pork and Vegetable Kabobs   40
Snapper Fillets   29
Southern Salmon Bowl   27
Spiced Red Snapper Fillet   25
Spicy Chicken Wings   102
Spicy Potato Chips   68
Spicy-Sweet Pork Tenderloin   106
Spinach and Ricotta Pockets   87
Stuffed Bell Peppers with Cream Cheese   54
Sweet Strawberry and Rhubarb Crumble   73
Sweet-Salty Mixed Snack   69
Sweet-Sour London Broil   35

T
Tangy Pork Ribs   40
Tangy Sweet Potatoes   63
Teriyaki Chicken Thighs with Snow Peas   49
Teriyaki Sauce   12
Thai Spicy Napa Vegetables   58
Thai Sweet-Sour Brussels Sprouts   56
Toasted Eggplant, Peppers, Garlic, and Onion   59
Toasted Rotisserie Pork Shoulder   108
Toasted Scallops with Mushrooms   31
Toasted Tofu, Carrot and Cauliflower Rice   57
Tomato Omelet with Avocado Dressing   22
Tuna Patties with Cheese Sauced   28

V
Vanilla Chocolate Cookies   73

CPSIA information can be obtained
at www.ICGtesting.com
Printed in the USA
LVHW100805010221
677982LV00011B/378